HANS MAGNUS ENZENSBERGER

NEW SELECTED POEMS

T0352415

HANS MAGNUS ENZENSBERGER

NEW SELECTED POEMS

TRANSLATED BY

DAVID CONSTANTINE
HANS MAGNUS ENZENSBERGER
MICHAEL HAMBURGER
ESTHER KINSKY

BLOODAXE BOOKS

ISBN: 978 1 78037 250 1

This edition first published 2015 by
Bloodaxe Books Ltd,
Eastburn,
South Park,
Hexham,
Northumberland NE46 1BS.

www.bloodaxebooks.com
For further information about Bloodaxe titles
please visit our website or write to
the above address for a catalogue.

Supported using public funding by
ARTS COUNCIL
ENGLAND

Cover design: Neil Astley & Pamela Robertson-Pearce.

Printed in Great Britain by Bell & Bain Limited, Glasgow, Scotland, on
acid-free paper sourced from mills with FSC chain of custody certification.

To the noble coolies of poetry,
translators in East and West,
with gratitude.

INHALT

CONTENTS

TRANSLATORS
DC   David Constantine
HME Hans Magnus Enzensberger
MH   Michael Hamburger
EK   Esther Kinsky

ACKNOWLEDGEMENTS

This edition reprints the whole of Hans Magnus Enzensberger's bilingual *Selected Poems*, translated by Hans Magnus Enzensberger and Michael Hamburger (Bloodaxe Books, 1994), which covers collections from *Landessprache* (Language of the Country, 1960) to *Zukunftsmusik* (Music of the Future, 1991). Some of the translations by Enzensberger were first published in *The Sinking of the Titanic* (Carcanet, 1981; Paladin, 1989). Some of the translations by Hamburger were first published in *Poems* (Northern House, 1966), *poems for people who don't read poems* (Secker & Warburg, 1968; Atheneum, New York, 1968) and *Selected Poems* (Penguin, 1968). Some previously uncollected translations were first published in *Poetry Review* and *Stand*. All the German texts are taken from editions published by Suhrkamp Verlag.

New Selected Poems also includes selections of poems from later collections published in German by Suhrkamp Verlag: *Kiosk: Neue Gedichte* (1993; *Kiosk*, translated by Michael Hamburger with additional translations by Enzensberger, Bloodaxe Books, 1995), *Leichter als Luft: Moralische Gedichte* (1999; *Lighter Than Air: moral poems*, translated by David Constantine with additional translations by Enzensberger, Bloodaxe Books, 2002), and *Die Geschichte der Wolken: 99 Meditationen* (2003; *A History of Clouds*: 99 *Meditations*, translated by Martin Chalmers and Esther Kinsky, Seagull Books, 2010). Special thanks are due to David Constantine for permission to reprint his translations and for his assistance with proofing, and to Kaveen Kishore, Martin Chalmers and Esther Kinsky for permission to include 'A History of Clouds' in this edition.

It should be noted also that where there are significant differences between Enzensberger's own translations and his German originals, these are not 'mistranslations' as some reviewers have mistakenly asserted, but either freer versions or examples of his wishing to continue writing the poem in English.

INTRODUCTION

In one way or another, as a poet, polemicist and commentator, Hans Magnus Enzensberger has been not only present, but conspicuous in the English-language countries for nearly twenty-five years, so that it seems unnecessary and impertinent to introduce him here. On the strength of his own brilliant English version of his major poem *The Sinking of the Titanic* alone, he could even qualify as an English-language poet. Since, for most of the time, he has also been an outstandingly public poet, far less concerned with his inner life than with matters he could assume to be immediately recognisable as common property, a biographical summary would be largely irrelevant and unhelpful. As for his public activities and involvements, the most condensed account of them would call for book-length treatment; and so would a key to his range of reference and allusion in the poems, of the kind he himself appended to his 'Summer Poem' and is best qualified to provide.

No Introduction was included in the first book selection of Enzensberger's poems, published in Britain and America in 1968, nor in the Northern House pamphlet that preceded it by two years. Characteristically Enzensberger's own title for the 1968 book was *poems for people who don't read poems*. An Introduction was added to the Penguin paperback edition of the same year, with the neutral and less provocative title *Selected Poems*.

Since that time Enzensberger has given up the lower case style he chose for the title of the book, as for its contents; and the provocative stance he had taken up in his first German collection of 1957, called *the wolves defended against the lambs*. His experience not only as a poet but as an editor, publisher, journalist, anthologist and translator of other people's poems in languages that range from Spanish to Norwegian, will have taught him that it matters very little what readers a poet has in mind for his poems – or did before advertising techniques became as dominant as they have become even in the arts. *poems for people who don't read poems* was read by the relatively small number of people who read poems. The prose books – as provocative and polemical as the early poems – that were to follow fairly regularly since 1962 may have been read by a rather larger number of people, though they came out of the same concerns.

If so, it was for the obvious reason that the reading of poems, not excluding anti-poems, is a habit and skill less widespread than the reading of prose, a medium shared with newspapers and the information industry.

From the first, Enzensberger's special function as a poet and prose writer arose from his awareness of being a West German just old enough to have received his early conditioning in the Third Reich, though he was only fifteen years old when it collapsed. Unlike many of his seniors and coevals, he was not content to blame the 'wolves' of an older generation for what that order had perpetrated. If he was to be the conscience of his own generation, as he was widely acknowledged to be in the sixties and seventies, he had to break with the conformism and the 'inwardness' – the moral alibi of so many of his predecessors – that had allowed the German 'lambs' to feel good while going to the slaughter, their own as well as that of those classified as goats. As recently as in his latest prose book, *Aussichten auf den Bürgerkrieg* (Prospects for Civil War) of 1993, Enzensberger insisted that the meekness of the lambs was and remains a prerequisite for every atrocity committed by the wolves. The peculiar tough-mindedness of his stance, always combined with the utmost elegance, is inseparable from that early recognition.

By tough-mindedness here I don't mean aggressiveness, though the incisive, abrasive rhetoric of his earliest poems was felt to be aggressive by many of his German readers. What I mean is that, in his compassion as much as in his quarrels with others, he has avoided appeals to emotions not tested by knowledge and intelligence; and the assumption, constant in his poems, that the survival of individuals, groups, nations and species has long ceased to be guaranteed, and can be achieved only if its defenders are as active, resourceful and resilient as those who endanger it.

As early as 1960, too, when he published a pioneering anthology of international modern poetry, he was prescient enough to call it a 'museum' – long before the term 'post-modernist' had gone into general – and dubious – circulation; and he explained why he considered modernism to be defunct in an essay included in his book *Einzelheiten* of 1962. What he renounced for himself – without disparaging its achievements – was the deliberate experimentation of former 'avant-gardes' – and the very notion of progress in the arts implied by the word itself. This did not absolve him from the need to write well; and, when his themes demanded it, he made use of modernist devices like the 'collage' or 'montage' structure of longer poems, from 'Lachesis Lapponica' and 'Summer Poem' onwards. Where such poems are difficult or demanding, it is because Enzensberger knows things most of his readers do not know, put in not for the sake of innovation or idiosyncracy but because in our time even public and moral issues cannot be adequately responded to in poetry without an awareness of their inherent complexities and contradictions. Whatever his themes – and Enzensberger's concerns were ecological, as well as social and political, almost from the start – Enzensberger has grappled with those complexities and contra-dictions, to the point of giving up poetry itself for a while, as a medium no longer capable of serving the cause of survival. That was at a time when West German literature had been politicised and ideologised to an extent that tended to make the personal de-cisions of an established writer exemplary and prescriptive, quite especially if he was a writer in the thick of all the controversies, as Enzensberger was at the time, not only as a poet but as the editor of the radical periodical *Kursbuch* (Railway Timetable!). This crisis and dilemma had to be overcome by distinguishing what had looked like a strictly political commitment from the moral commitment much more compatible with good imaginative writing, whether in prose or verse. The turning-point came with Enzensberger's stay in Cuba in 1969, during which he began work on *The Sinking of The Titanic*, first published in Germany in 1978. His Cuban exper-iences were woven into the broken narrative of that poem, together with many other layers, seeming interpolations, digressions, leaps in space, time and even manner.

Enzensberger's modernity – as distinct from modernism – lies in his exceptional grasp of the pluralism of our age. His work em-bodies the multiple awareness with which all of us are cursed by the sheer quantity and instant transmission of information, disaster, scandal, sensation, selected news of the world. It has been Enzens-berger's distinction not to have recoiled from this battery of appeals to our interest, sympathy, anger and outrage, but to have gone out of his way to be more widely informed than most of the more specialised transmitters – about science and technology as much as the most diverse societies, their economics and politics, not to mention linguistics, history and the arts. At one time, I remember, he went so far as to purge his library of 'belles-lettres', in favour of reference books, manuals, treatises and factual reports. He was so shocked to find that I made do with a long superseded printing of the Concise Oxford English Dictionary that he gave me a copy of the Shorter Oxford English Dictionary, still in use, with the inscription: 'eine hand voll wort-futter für die vögel in michaels kopf' – 'a handful of word-feed for the bats in Michael's belfry.' If the bats in my belfry were only fattened by that food, the likelihood of that outcome was implicit in the inscription. Radical though he used to be, Enzensberger has never been simplistic.

This Bloodaxe selection includes all the poems translated by Enzensberger himself or by me for the early pamphlet and books, together with our uncollected later translations and his own extracts from his book-length poem. His latest German collection, *Zukunfts-musik* (1991) is so different from his earlier work that it does seem to call for something in the way of introduction, if only because it may be felt to contradict the little I have written here about his work in general.

Lateness, in fact, marks not only the manner but the themes of these poems; and the change is as much a personal one, a sense of one man's time running out, as a political and cultural one, since in his poems Enzensberger has always merged personal concerns in general ones. Several of the poems in the first section of the book have to do with paintings and painters, all the poems in the book with ways of looking. Enzensberger's increasingly historical perspective on art links up with earlier work in his book of prose poems *Mausoleum* of 1975 and in the collection *Die Furie des Verschwindens* (The Fury of Disappearance) of 1980, much as the second section links up with the sociological preoccupations that were prominent in his work from the start.

What has changed is Enzensberger's stance. The same poet who could once claim to write poems for people who don't read poems will be neither understood or appreciated now by any reader whose mind and ear are not receptive to the most delicate modulations of the medium; and even such readers could find Enzensberger's late manner deficient in immediacy and the sensuousness which Milton thought essential to the language of poetry. It isn't only that the new poems are less direct and unambiguous. The difficulty – for English readers especially, with their preference for identifiable particulars of situation, scene or person, for referential images – has to do with a degree of abstraction that some will think more suitable in the visual arts and music than in poetry.

In Enzensberger's recent prose books, too, his stance has changed from one of mundane and differentiated partiality to one of amused, benign and impartial detachment. In the late poems his scepticism extends to the diction as much as to the message; and his wit has ceased to be a weapon with a single edge. The precision of the late poems is due less to a command of language and idiom, to his old eloquence, than to a questioning of them. The character studies still prominent in *Die Furie des Verschwindens*, too, have given way to an intense questioning of what and how we speak, what and how we perceive. Though the same material is drawn upon – the wide experience and interests of a lifetime – it is presented much more hesitantly, probingly and searchingly, without the early Enzensberger's assurance of a representative function. The social and moral criticism of the earlier books of poems has become existential, almost metaphysical in places.

Ageing itself may have a good deal to do with the change. The ironic title of the book – *Music of the Future* – is a more telling pointer, because both past and future are more operative in these poems than Enzensberger's earlier responses to topical issues; and no contemplation of the future now is conducive to the certainties that has sustained his polemics in verse and prose. The title poem, the last in the book and not among those we had translated, evokes a music of the future that is more like a silence:

> That which we can't wait for
> will show us.
> It gleams, is uncertain, remote.
>
> That which we let come towards us,
> does not await us,
> does not come towards us,
> does not come back to us,
> stands off.
>
> Does not belong to us,
> does not enquire about us,
> doesn't want to know about us,
> tells us nothing,
> is not our due.

Was not,
is not there for us,
has never been there,
is never there,
is never.

This is a poetry less of enactment than of evaluation, and a poetry of bare bones. The few adjectives in it carry more weight than adjectives usually do in poems; and these adjectives take on a character more metaphorical than descriptive or decorative. Once again it is a rare advantage to English-speaking readers that Enzensberger was able and willing to contribute his own versions of poems so bare as to be barely translatable.

MICHAEL HAMBURGER

This introductory essay was originally published in *Selected Poems* (1994).

LANGUAGE OF THE COUNTRY
LANDESSPRACHE

(1960)

Landessprache

*Ostendebat namque varium iracundum iniustum
inconstantem eundem exorabilem clementem
misericordem gloriosum excelsum humilem
ferocem fugacemque et omnia pariter.*

PLINIUS, Hist. nat. XXXV, XXXVI.

Was habe ich hier verloren,
in diesem Land,
dahin mich gebracht haben meine Älteren
durch Arglosigkeit?
Eingeboren, doch ungetrost,
abwesend bin ich hier,
ansässig im gemütlichen Elend,
in der netten, zufriedenen Grube.

Was habe ich hier? und was habe ich hier zu suchen,
in dieser Schlachtschüssel, diesem Schlaraffenland,
wo es aufwärts geht, aber nicht vorwärts,
wo der Überdruß ins bestickte Hungertuch beißt,
wo in den Delikateßgeschäften die Armut, kreidebleich,
mit erstickter Stimme aus dem Schlagrahm röchelt und ruft:
es geht aufwärts!
wo eine Gewinnspanne weit von den armen Reichen die reichen
        Armen
vor Begeisterung ihre Kinostühle zerschmettern,
da geht es aufwärts von Fall zu Fall,
wo die Zahlungsbilanz Hosianna und alles was recht ist singt
und ruft: das ist nicht genug,
daß da die Freizeit spurt und Gas gibt und hinhaut,
das ist das kleinere Übel, das ist nur die Hälfte,
das macht nichts, das ist nicht genug,
daß die Tarifpartner durch die Straßen irren
und mit geballten Fäusten frohlocken
und singen und sagen:

hier geht es aufwärts,
hier ist gut sein,
wo es rückwärts aufwärts geht,

Language of the Country

He displayed them as fickle, choleric, unjust
and variable, but also placable and merciful
and compassionate, boastful, lofty and humble,
fierce and timid – and all these at the same time.
PLINY, Natural History XXXV, XXXVI.

What am I doing here,
in this country
to which my elders brought me
intending no harm?
Native but comfortless
absently I am here,
settled in cosy squalor,
in this nice, contented hole.

What do I have here? What business
in this bean feast, this never-never-land
where things are looking up but getting nowhere,
where surfeited hunger chews the embroidered napkin,
where in delicatessen shops poverty, white as chalk,
with stifled voice gasps through whipped cream, and calls out
things are looking up!
Where a profit margin away from the poor rich the rich poor
smash their cinema seats for sheer joy
because things are looking up, more so every day,
where the balance of payments and fair enough sing
and call out: it is not enough
that leisure booms and steps on the gas and gets going,
this is the lesser evil, this is only one half,
this makes no difference, this is not enough,
that the wage negotiators wander lost in the streets
and with clenched fists rejoice
and sing and proclaim:

here things are looking up,
all's right with the world
where things are looking up backwards,

hier schießt der leitende Herr den leitenden Herrn mit dem Gesangbuch ab,
hier führen die Leichtbeschädigten mit den Schwerbeschädigten Krieg,
hier heißt es unerbittlich nett zueinander sein,

und das ist das kleinere Übel,
das wundert mich nicht,
das nehmen die Käufer in Kauf,
hier, wo eine Hand die andere kauft,
Hand aufs Herz, hier sind wir zuhaus,

hier laßt uns Hütten bauen,
auf diesem arischen Schrotthaufen,
auf diesem krächzenden Parkplatz,
wo aus den Ruinen Ruinen sprossen,
nagelneu, Ruinen auf Vorrat, auf Raten,
auf Abruf, auf Widerruf:

Hiersein ist herrlich,
wo dem verbrauchten Verbraucher,
und das ist das kleinere Übel,
die Haare ausfallen,
wo er sein erfolgreiches Haupt verhüllt
mit Wellpappe und Cellophan,
wo er abwesend aus der Grube ruft:
hier laßt uns Hütten bauen,

in dieser Mördergrube,
wo der Kalender sich selber abreißt vor Ohnmacht und Hast,
wo die Vergangenheit in den Müllschluckern schwelt
und die Zukunft mit falschen Zähnen knirscht,
das kommt davon, daß es aufwärts geht,
da tun wir Fleckenwasser drauf,
das ist hier so üblich, das wundert mich nicht,

goldrichtig liegen wir hier,
wo das Positive zum Höchstkurs notiert,
die Handelskammern decken sich damit ein
und bahren es auf unter Panzerglas,

here hymnbooks decide what boss will be picked by the bosses,
here the partly disabled wage war against the wholly disabled,
here the rule is: be ruthlessly nice to each other,

and this is the lesser evil,
this does not surprise me,
this the bargainers bargain with,
here, where one hand buys the other,
cross my heart, shake hands, here we're at home,

here let us build tabernacles,
on this Ayran dump of scrap,
where from ruins ruins sprout
brand new, ruins in stock,
ruins by standing order,
by instalments, sale or return:

To be here is glorious,
where the consumptive consumer,
and this is the lesser evil,
loses his hair,
where he hides his successful head
under cardboard and plastic bags,
where absently he calls out from the hole:
here let us build tabernacles

in this murderers' den
where in haste and impotence the calendar tears its own leaves,
where the past rots and reeks in the rubbish disposal unit
and the future grits its false teeth,
that's all because things are looking up,
we treat it with stain removers,
that's our custom here, this does not surprise me,

right as gold we lie here
where positive values are quoted at peak prices,
the chambers of commerce lay in stock
and lay it out in state under bulletproof glass,

wo wir uns finden wohl unter Blinden,
in den Schau-, Kauf- und Zeughäusern,
und das ist nicht alles, das ist nur die Hälfte,
das ist die tiefgefrorene Wildnis,
das ist die erfolgreiche Raserei, das tanzt
im notdürftigen Nerz, auf zerbrochenen Knien,
im ewigen Frühling der Amnesie,
das ist ein anderes Land als andere Länder,
das reut mich, und daß es mich reut,
das ist das kleinere Übel, denn das ist wahr,
was seine Opfer, ganz gewöhnliche tote Leute,
aus der Erde rufen, etwas Laut – und Erfolgloses,
das an das schalldichte Pflaster dringt
von unten, und es beschlägt, daß es dunkel wird,
fleckig, naß, bis eine Lache,
eine ganz gewöhnliche Lache es überschwemmt,

und den Butzemann überschwemmt,
das Löweneckerchen, das Allerleirauh,
und die schöne Rapunzel, die sind nicht mehr hier,
und es gibt keine Städte mehr, und keine Fische,
die sind erstickt in dieser Lache,

wie meine Brüder, die tadel – und hilflosen Pendler,
wie sie mich reuen, die frommen Gerichtsvollzieher,
die Gasmänner, wie sie waten zuhauf,
mit ihren Plombierzangen, wie sie stapfen,
mit ihren abwesenden Stiefeln, durchs Bodenlose,
die Gloriole vorschriftsmäßig tief im Genick:

ja wären's Leute wie andere Leute,
war es ein ganz gewöhnliches, ein andres
als dieses Nacht- und Nebelland,
von Abwesenden überfüllt,
die wer sie sind nicht wissen noch wissen wollen,
die in dieses Land geraten sind
auf der Flucht vor diesem Land
und werden flüchtig sein bis zur Grube:

where on the bonny bonny banks we play blind man's buff,
in exhibition rooms, arsenals, sale rooms,
and this is not all, this is only one half,
this is the frozen-up waste,
this is successful madness, this dances
in needy mink, on broken knees,
in amnesia's eternal springtime,
this is a country different from any other,
this makes me remorseful, and this remorse of mine
is the lesser evil, for this is the truth
which its victims, people quite ordinary and dead,
call out from under the earth, something soundless and unsuccessful,
something that beats against the soundproof pavement
from down below and dims it, so it grows dark,
spotty, wet, till a puddle,
a puddle quite ordinary spreads where it was,

and covers the fairy tale dwarf,
the larch tree, little grey mouse
and lovely Rapunzel, these are no longer here,
and there are no cities left, and no fishes,
these have choked in that puddle,

like my brothers, the blameless and helpless commuters,
how remorseful they make me, the pious bailiffs,
the gasmen, how they wade all together,
with their seals and pincers, how they stamp
in their absent boots, over the bottomless places,
their statutory haloes low on their necks:

all right, if these were people like any others,
if it were a quite ordinary country,
different from this land of night and mist
overcrowded with absent people
who neither know nor want to know who they are,
who have come to this country
on their flight from this country
and will be in flight till they're buried:

wärs anders, wär ihm zu helfen,
wäre Rat und Genugtuung hier,
wär es nicht dieses brache, mundtote Feindesland!

Was habe ich hier verloren, was suche ich
und stochre in diesem unzuständigen Knäuel
von Nahkampfspangen, Genußscheinen,
Gamsbärten, Schlußverkäufen, und finde nichts
als chronische, chronologisch geordnete Turnhallen
und Sachbearbeiter für die Menschlichkeit
in den Kasernen für die Kasernen für die Kasernen:

Was soll ich hier? und was soll ich sagen?
in welcher Sprache? und wem?
Da tut mir die Wahl weh wie ein Messerstich,
das reut mich, das ist das kleinere Übel,
das schreit und so weiter
mit kleinen Schreien zum Himmel
und gibt sich für größer aus als es ist,
aber es ist nicht ganz,
es ist nur die himmelschreiende Hälfte,
es ist noch nicht genug:

denn dieses Land, vor Hunger rasend,
zerrauft sich sorgfältig mit eigenen Händen,
dieses Land ist von sich selber geschieden,
ein aufgetrenntes, inwendig geschiedenes Herz,
unsinnig tickend, eine Bombe aus Fleisch,
eine nasse, abwesende Wunde:

Deutschland, mein Land, unheilig Herz der Völker,
ziemlich verrufen, von Fall zu Fall,
unter allen gewöhnlichen Leuten:

Meine zwei Länder und ich, wir sind geschiedene Leute,
und doch bin ich inständig hier,
in Asche und Sack, und frage mich:
was habe ich hier verloren?

if it were different it could be helped,
there'd be comfort and satisfaction,
if it were not this fallow, silenced and hostile land.

What am I doing here, why do I try
to undo this incompetent tangle
of close combat bars, of bonus vouchers,
chamois beard hats, closing down sales, and find nothing
but chronic, chronologically graded gymnasiums
and specialists in charge of humanity
in barracks for barracks for barracks:

What's my purpose here? and what shall I say?
in what language? to whom?
this decision hurts like the stab of a knife,
this makes me remorseful, this is the lesser evil
this screams and so forth
with little screams up to heaven
and pretends to be bigger than it is,
but it is not the whole,
it is only one half crying out to heaven,
it still is not enough:

for this country, raving with hunger,
carefully tears itself to pieces with its own hands,
this country is divided from itself,
a rent, an inwardly divided heart
senselessly ticking, a bomb made of flesh,
a wet, an absent wound:

Germany, my country, unholy heart of the nations,
pretty notorious, more so every day,
among ordinary people elsewhere:

my two countries and I, we've gone separate ways,
and yet I am wholly here
in sackcloth and ashes, and ask:
what is my business here?

Das habe ich hier verloren,
was auf meiner Zunge schwebt,
etwas andres, das Ganze,
das furchtlos scherzt mit der ganzen Welt
und nicht in dieser Lache ertrinkt,

verloren an dieses fremde, geschiedne Geröchel,
das gepreßte Geröchel im *Neuen Deutschland*,
das *Frankfurter Allgemeine* Geröchel
(und das ist das kleinere Übel),
ein mundtotes Würgen, das nichts von sich weiß,
von dem ich nichts wissen will, Musterland,
Mördergrube, in die ich herzlich geworfen bin
bei halbwegs lebendigem Leib,
da bleibe ich jetzt,
ich hadere aber ich weiche nicht,
da bleibe ich eine Zeitlang,
bis ich von hinnen fahre zu den anderen Leuten,
und ruhe aus, in einem ganz gewöhnlichen Land,
hier nicht,
nicht hier.

My business here is with that
which hovers on my tongue,
something different, the whole,
that fearlessly, gaily consorts with the whole world
and does not drown in the puddle,

lost to this alien divided gasping,
the stifled gasping in our *New Germany,*
the *Frankfurter Allgemeine* gasping
(and this is the lesser evil)
a silenced groan that knows nothing about itself,
about which I want to know nothing, model country,
murderers' den into which I've been heartily thrown
half living still, half alive,
there I am staying now,
I grumble but do not budge,
there I shall stay for a time,
till I move on to the other people
and rest, in a country quite ordinary,
elsewhere,
not here.

Das Ende der Eulen

Ich spreche von euerm nicht,
ich spreche vom Ende der Eulen.
Ich spreche von Butt und Wal
in ihrem dunkeln Haus,
dem siebenfältigen Meer,
von den Gletschern,
sie werden kalben zu früh,
Rab und Taube, gefiederten Zeugen,
von allem was lebt in Lüften
und Wäldern, und den Flechten im Kies,
vom Weglosen selbst, und vom grauen Moor
und den leeren Gebirgen:

Auf Radarschirmen leuchtend
zum letzten Mal, ausgewertet
auf Meldetischen, von Antennen
tödlich befingert Floridas Sümpfe
und das sibirische Eis, Tier
und Schilf und Schiefer erwürgt
von Warnketten, umzingelt
vom letzten Manöver, arglos
unter schwebenden Feuerglocken,
im Ticken des Ernstfalls.

Wir sind schon vergessen.
Sorgt euch nicht um die Waisen,
aus dem Sinn schlagt euch
die mündelsichern Gefühle,
den Ruhm, die rostfreien Psalmen.
Ich spreche nicht mehr von euch,
Planern der spurlosen Tat,
und von mir nicht, und keinem.
Ich spreche von dem was nicht spricht,
von den sprachlosen Zeugen,
von Ottern und Robben,
von den alten Eulen der Erde.

The End of Owls

I do not speak of what's yours,
I speak of the end of the owls.
I speak of turbot and whale
in their glimmering house,
in the sevenfold sea,
of the glaciers –
too soon they will calve –
raven and dove, the feathered witnesses,
of all that lives in the winds
and woods, and the lichen on rock,
of impassable tracts and the grey moors
and the empty mountain ranges:

Shining on radar screens
for the last time, recorded,
checked out on consoles, fingered
by aerials fatally Florida's marshes
and the Siberian ice, animal,
reed and slate all strangled
by interlinked warnings, encircled
by the last manoeuvres, guileless
under hovering cones of fire,
while the time-fuses tick.

As for us, we're forgotten.
Don't give a thought to the orphans,
expunge from your minds
your gilt-edged security feelings
and fame and the stainless psalms.
I don't speak of you any more,
planners of vanishing actions,
nor of me, nor of anyone.
I speak of that without speech,
of the unspeaking witnesses,
of otters and seals,
of the ancient owls of the earth.

Die Hebammen

In brausenden Trauben schwärmen sie aus,
wenn der Morgen graut, klettern
über Hecken und Brücken behend
und belagern die fernsten Gehöfte.

Ihre prallen glänzenden Koffer drohn
wie schwarze Bomben, glimmend
auf Gletschern und Bahnsteigen,
Mooren, Hopfenfeldern und Riffen.

Die Nüstern der Ammen blähn sich vor Gier:
Wo es nach heißen Handtüchern riecht,
springen sie unverhofft querfeldein,
drücken knurrend die Türen auf
und werfen sich über die Betten.

Sie reißen ein Fleisch zur Welt,
das wenig wiegt, ein weißes Fleisch,
das ein paar dutzendmal überwintert:
dann ist es hin, und sie zerren
ans Licht einen Zornschrei,
der, wenn es Mittag wird, schallt
durch die Steinbrüche und erstickt
in einem Gewölk bleicher Windeln.

Dann, gegen Abend, sieht sie der Mond
bei ihren blutigen Zangen und Nadeln
und Scheren kauern, lahm, im Moos,
wie schlaflose Raben, frösteln,
starren in den weglosen kahlen
Straßengraben der nahenden Nacht.

The Midwives

In buzzing clusters out they swarm
in the grey light of daybreak clamber
limberly over hedges and bridges
and lay siege to remotest homesteads.

Their taut and gleaming toolbags threaten
like black time-bombs, glimmering
on glaciers and railway platforms,
on moors and hopfields and sandbanks.

The midwives' nostrils distend with greed:
wherever it smells of hot towels
cross-country they skip unforeseen,
push open doors with a growl
and hurl themselves at the bedsteads.

Into the world they rip
flesh that weighs little, white flesh
that survives a few dozen winters:
then it's done for; they drag
to the light a furious roar
which, towards noon, rings out
through the quarries and fades away,
choked in a cloud of pale napkins.

Later the moon sees them crouch
over bloody forceps and needles
and scissors, lame, in the moss
like sleepless ravens, chilly,
stare at the pathless blank
ditch of the oncoming night.

BRAILLE
BLINDENSCHRIFT
(1964)

Küchenzettel

An einem müßigen Nachmittag, heute
seh ich in meinem Haus
durch die offene Küchentür
eine Milchkanne   ein Zwiebelbrett
einen Katzenteller.
Auf dem Tisch liegt ein Telegramm.
Ich habe es nicht gelesen.

In einem Museum zu Amsterdam
sah ich auf einem alten Bild
durch die offene Küchentür
eine Milchkanne   einen Brotkorb
einen Katzenteller.
Auf dem Tisch lag ein Brief.
Ich habe ihn nicht gelesen.

In einem Sommerhaus an der Moskwa
sah ich vor wenig Wochen
durch die offene Küchentür
einen Brotkorb   ein Zwiebelbrett
einen Katzenteller.
Auf dem Tisch lag die Zeitung.
Ich habe sie nicht gelesen.

Durch die offene Küchentür
seh ich vergossene Milch
Dreißigjährige Kriege
Tränen auf Zwiebelbrettern
Anti-Raketen-Raketen
Brotkörbe
Klassenkämpfe.

Links unten ganz in der Ecke
seh ich einen Katzenteller.

Bill of Fare

One idle afternoon, today
in my house I see
through the open kitchen door
a milk jug   a chopping board
a plate for the cat.
A telegram lies on the table
I have not read it.

In a museum at Amsterdam
in an old picture I saw
through the open kitchen door
a milk jug   a bread basket
a plate for the cat.
A letter lay on the table.
I have not read it.

In a dacha on the Moskwa
a few weeks ago I saw
through the open kitchen door
a bread basket   a chopping board
a plate for the cat.
A newspaper lay on the table
I have not read it.

Through the open kitchen door
I see spilt milk
Thirty Years' wars
tears on chopping boards
anti-rocket rockets
bread baskets
class wars.

Low down in the left corner
I see a plate for the cat.

Abgelegenes Haus

(für Günter Eich)

Wenn ich erwache
schweigt das Haus.
Nur die Vögel lärmen.
Ich sehe aus dem Fenster
niemand. Hier

führt keine Straße vorbei.
Es ist kein Draht am Himmel
und kein Draht in der Erde.
Ruhig liegt das Lebendige
unter dem Beil.

Ich setze das Wasser auf.
Ich schneide mein Brot.
Unruhig drücke ich
auf den roten Knopf
des kleinen Transistors.

»Karibische Krise…wäscht weißer
und weißer und weißer…
einsatzbereit…Stufe drei…
That's the way I love you…
Montanwerte kräftig erholt…«

Ich nehme nicht das Beil.
Ich schlage das Gerät nicht in Stücke.
Die Stimme des Schreckens
beruhigt mich, sie sagt:
Wir sind noch am Leben.

Das Haus schweigt.
Ich weiß nicht, wie man Fallen stellt
und eine Axt macht aus Flintstein,
wenn die letzte Schneide
verrostet ist.

Remote House

(for Günter Eich)

When I wake up
the house is silent.
Only the birds make a noise.
Through the window I see
no one. Here

no road passes.
There is no wire in the sky
and no wire in the earth.
Quiet the living things lie
under the axe.

I put water on to boil.
I cut my bread.
Unquiet I press
the red push-button
of the small transistor.

'Caribbean crisis…washes whiter
and whiter and whiter…troops ready to fly out…
phase three… *that's the way I love you…*
amalgamated steel stocks are back to par…'

I do not take the axe.
I do not smash the gadget to pieces.
The voice of terror
calms me; it says:
We are still alive.

The house is silent.
I do not know how to set traps
or make an axe out of flint,
when the last blade
has rusted.

Camera obscura

In meinen vier vorläufigen Wänden
aus Fichtenholz
vier mal fünf mal zweieinhalb Meter
in meinem winzigen Zimmer
bin ich allein

allein mit dem Bratapfel, der Dunkelheit,
der Sechzig-Watt-Birne,
mit der Bundeswehr, mit der Eule
allein

mit dem Briefbeschwerer aus blauem Glas,
der Kybernetik, dem Tod,
mit der Stuckrosette
allein

mit dem Gottseibeiuns
und dem Weiherweg in Kaufbeuren
(Reg. Bez. Schwaben)
mit meiner Milz allein

mit meinem Gevatter Rabmüller,
vor zwanzig Jahren vergast,
allein mit dem roten Telefon,
und mit vielem, was ich mir merken will.

Allein mit Krethi und Plethi,
Bouvard und Pécuchet,
Kegel und Kind,
Pontius und Pilatus.

In meinem unendlichen Zimmer
vier mal fünf mal zweieinhalb Meter
bin ich allein mit einem Spiralnebel
von Bildern

Camera Obscura

Within my four provisional walls
of firwood
twelve by twelve by seven feet
in my diminutive room
I am alone

alone with baked apples, the dark,
the sixty-watt bulb,
the federal army, the owl
alone

with the paperweight of blue glass,
with cybernetics, with death,
with the plaster rosette
alone

with Old Nick
and the pondside lane at Kaufbeuren
(Admin. Reg. Suabia)
alone with my spleen

with my godfather Rabmüller,
gassed twenty years ago,
alone with the red telephone
and with much that I want to remember.

Alone with Tom, Dick and Harry,
Bouvard and Pécuchet,
with kith and kin and chattels,
Pontius and Pilate.

In my infinite room
twelve by twelve by seven feet
I am alone with a spiral nebula
of images

von Bildern von Bildern
von Bildern von Bildern von Bildern
enzyklopädisch und leer
und unzweifelhaft

allein mit meinem vorläufigen Gehirn
darin ich wiederfinde den Bratapfel,
die Dunkelheit, den Gevatter Rabmüller,
und vieles was ich vergessen will.

of images of images
of images of images of images
encyclopaedic and empty
and not to be doubted

alone with my provisional brain
in which I discover baked apples,
the dark, my godfather Rabmüller
and much that I want to forget.

Ufer

Am andern Ufer, im grauen Morgen
entscheidet sich wer ich bin
in einem Rauch.

Ich rieche den Hanf hier, den Teer,
das verwitterte Holz.
Anderswo sind die andern.

Der Bootssteg zittert,
aber die Schritte
tragen nicht weit.

Es ist wenig zu sehen.

Draußen im Wasser treibt etwas,
etwas Bleiches treibt ab.
Rümpfe von Bäumen, von Kähnen,
von Männern.

Ruf nur, sage ich, ruf
mit deiner bleichen Stimme,
die Worte tragen nicht weit
in einem Rauch.

Am andern Ufer,
immer am andern Ufer
entscheidet sich was das ist:
dieser Hanf, dies Holz,
dieser verwitterte Schrei.

Gibt es ein anderes Ufer?

Nichts überhole ich.
Nichts holt mich über.
Nichts entscheidet sich hier.
Hier herrscht eine große Ruhe.

Shore

On the other shore, in the grey morning
what I am is decided
in a haze of smoke.

I smell the hemp here, the tar,
the mouldering wood.
The others are elsewhere.

The landing-stage quivers
but my steps
do not take me far.

There isn't much one can see.

Out in the water something drifts.
Something pale drifts away.
Stumps of trees, of boats,
of men.

Cry out, then, I say.
Cry out with your pale voice.
The words will not go far
in a haze of smoke.

On the other shore,
always the other shore
what these are is decided:
this hemp, this wood,
this mouldering cry.

Is there another shore?

I overtake nothing.
Nothing takes me over.
Nothing is decided here.
Here a great stillness reigns.

Es ist wenig zu sehen.

Langsam trocknet der Hanf
in einem Rauch.

There isn't much one can see.

Slowly the hemp dries
in a haze of smoke.

Der Andere

Einer lacht
kümmert sich
hält mein Gesicht mit Haut und Haar unter den Himmel
läßt Wörter rollen aus meinem Mund
einer der Geld und Angst und einen Paß hat
einer der streitet und liebt
einer rührt sich
einer zappelt

aber nicht ich
Ich bin der andere
der nicht lacht
der kein Gesicht unter dem Himmel hat
und keine Wörter in seinem Mund
der unbekannt ist mit sich und mit mir
nicht ich: der Andere: immer der Andere
der nicht siegt noch besiegt wird
der sich nicht kümmert
der sich nicht rührt

der Andere
der sich gleichgültig ist
von dem ich nicht weiß
von dem niemand weiß wer er ist
der mich nicht rührt
das bin ich

The Other

One laughs
is worried
under the sky exposes my face and my hair
makes words roll out of my mouth
one who has money and fears and a passport
one who quarrels and loves
one moves
one struggles

but not I
I am the other
who does not laugh
who has no face to expose to the sky
and no words in his mouth
who is unacquainted with me with himself
not I: the other: always the other
who neither wins nor loses
who is not worried
who does not move

the other
indifferent to himself
of whom I know nothing
of whom nobody knows who he is
who does not move me
that is I

Auf das Grab eines friedlichen Mannes

Dieser da war kein Menschenfreund,
mied Versammlungen, Kaufhäuser, Arenen.
Seinesgleichen Fleisch aß er nicht.

Auf den Straßen ging die Gewalt
lächelnd, nicht nackt.
Aber es waren Schreie am Himmel.

Die Gesichter der Leute waren nicht deutlich.
Sie schienen zertrümmert,
noch ehe der Schlag gefallen war.

Eines, um das er zeitlebens gekämpft hat,
mit Wörtern und Zähnen, ingrimmig,
hinterlistig, auf eigene Faust:

das Ding, das er seine Ruhe nannte
da er es hat, nun ist kein Mund mehr
an seinem Gebein, es zu schmecken.

For the Grave of a Peace-loving Man

This one was no philanthropist,
avoided meetings, stadiums, the large stores.
Did not eat the flesh of his own kind.

Violence walked the streets,
smiling, not naked.
But there were screams in the sky.

People's faces were not very clear.
They seemed to be battered
even before the blow had struck home.

One thing for which he fought all his life,
with words, tooth and claw, grimly,
cunningly, off his own bat:

the thing which he called his peace,
now that he's got it, there is no longer a mouth
over his bones, to taste it with.

Middle Class Blues

Wir können nicht klagen.
Wir haben zu tun.
Wir sind satt.
Wir essen.

Das Gras wächst,
das Sozialprodukt,
der Fingernagel,
die Vergangenheit.

Die Straßen sind leer.
Die Abschlüsse sind perfekt.
Die Sirenen schweigen.
Das geht vorüber.

Die Toten haben ihr Testament gemacht.
Der Regen hat nachgelassen.
Der Krieg ist noch nicht erklärt.
Das hat keine Eile.

Wir essen das Gras.
Wir essen das Sozialprodukt.
Wir essen die Fingernägel.
Wir essen die Vergangenheit.

Wir haben nichts zu verheimlichen.
Wir haben nichts zu versäumen.
Wir haben nichts zu sagen.
Wir haben.

Die Uhr ist aufgezogen.
Die Verhältnisse sind geordnet.
Die Teller sind abgespült.
Der letzte Autobus fährt vorbei.

Middle Class Blues

We can't complain.
We're not out of work.
We don't go hungry.
We eat.

The grass grows,
the social product,
the fingernail,
the past.

The streets are empty.
The deals are closed.
The sirens are silent.
All that will pass.

The dead have made their wills.
The rain's become a drizzle.
The war's not yet been declared.
There's no hurry for that.

We eat the grass.
We eat the social product.
We eat the fingernails.
We eat the past.

We have nothing to conceal.
We have nothing to miss.
We have have nothing to say.
We have.

The watch has been wound up.
The bills have been paid.
The washing-up has been done.
The last bus is passing by.

Er ist leer.

Wir können nicht klagen.

Worauf warten wir noch?

It is empty.

We can't complain.

What are we waiting for?

Bildnis eines Spitzels

Im Supermarkt lehnt er
unter der Plastiksonne,
die weißen Flecken in seinem Gesicht
sind Wut, nicht Schwindsucht,
hundert Schachteln Knuspi-Knackers
(*weil sie so herzhaft sind*)
zündet er mit den Augen an,
ein Stück Margarine
(die gleiche Marke wie ich:
Goldlux, weil sie so lecker ist)
nimmt er in seine feuchte Hand
und zerdrückt sie zu Saft.

Er ist neunundzwanzig,
hat Sinn für das Höhere,
schläft schlecht und allein
mit Broschüren und Mitessern,
haßt den Chef und den Supermarkt,
die Kommunisten, die Weiber,
die Hausbesitzer, sich selbst
und seine zerbissenen Fingernägel
voll Margarine (*weil sie
so lecker ist*), brabbelt
unter der Künstlerfrisur
vor sich hin wie ein Greis.

Der
wird es nie zu was bringen.
Schnittler, glaube ich, heißt er,
Schnittler, Hittler, oder so ähnlich.

Portrait of a House Detective

He lolls in the supermarket
under the plastic sun,
the white patches on his face
are rage, not consumption,
a hundred packets of crispy crackers
(*because they're so nourishing*)
he sets ablaze with his eyes,
a piece of margarine
(the same brand as mine:
goldlux, because it's so delicious)
he picks up with his moist hand
and squeezes it till it drips.

He's twenty-nine,
idealistic,
sleeps badly and alone
with brochures and blackheads,
hates the boss and the supermarket,
communists, women,
landlords, himself
and his bitten fingernails
full of margarine (*because
it's so delicious*), under
his arty hairstyle mutters
to himself like a pensioner.

That one
will never get anywhere.
Wittler, I think, he's called,
Wittler, Hittler, or something like that.

Purgatorio

Wehe die Erde ist winzig auf den Broschüren
Zur Snackbar watscheln Entwicklungshelfer
eingewickelt in Reiseschecks
Die Quarantäneflagge ist aufgezogen

Herr Albert Schweitzer
wird zur Transit-Auskunft gebeten

Ausgebuchte Buchhalter rudern
durch gläserne Korridore
zum Jüngsten Gericht
Letzter Abruf nach Nagasaki

Herr Adolf Eichmann
wird zur Transit-Auskunft gebeten

Die Welt ist wegen Nebels geschlossen
auf Tretrollern fahren Bräute vor
in wehenden Totenhemden
Die Maschine ist startbereit

Monsieur Godot
wird zur Transit-Auskunft gebeten

Ausgang B Position zweiunddreißig
Die Nylonstimme ruft Weh über uns
Leichenzüge fluten über die Pisten
In der Dunkelheit flammen Sirenen

Purgatorio

Woe the earth is tiny in the brochures
To the snackbar waddle development experts
enveloped in travel cheques
The quarantine flag has been hoisted

Will Herr Albert Schweitzer
please go to Transit Information

Booked out book-keepers paddle
through glass-lined corridors
to the last judgement
Last call for Nagasaki

Will Herr Adolf Eichmann
please go to Transit Information

On account of fog the world is closed
On pedal trolleys brides arrive
in shrouds that trail in the wind
The plane is ready to take off

Will Monsieur Godot
please go to Transit Information

Exit B Channel thirty-two
The nylon voice cries woe upon us
Funeral processions flood the runways
Sirens blaze in the dark

Historischer Prozeß

Die Bucht ist zugefroren.
Die Fischkutter liegen fest.
Das besagt nichts.
Du bist frei.
Du kannst dich hinstrecken.
Du kannst wieder aufstehen.
Es ist nicht schade um deinen Namen.
Du kannst verschwinden
und wiederkommen.
Das ist möglich.
Auch wenn einer stirbt
kommen noch Briefe für ihn.
Es ist nicht viel zu vereiteln.
Du kannst schlafen.
Das ist möglich.
Über Nacht wird der Eisbrecher da sein.
Dann laufen die Kutter aus.
Die Fahrtrinne ist schmal.
Über Nacht friert sie wieder zu.
Das besagt nichts.
Es ist nicht schade um deinen Namen.

Historical Process

The bay is frozen up.
The trawlers are ice-bound.
So what.
You are free.
You can lie down.
You can get up again.
It doesn't matter about your name.
You can disappear
and return.
That's possible.
A fighter howls across the island.
Even when a man dies
letters still come for him.
There isn't much to be lost or thwarted.
You can sleep.
That's possible.
The ice-breaker will be here by the morning.
Then the trawlers will leave.
The channel they follow is narrow.
It freezes up again by the morning.
So what.
It doesn't matter about your name.

Karl Heinrich Marx

Riesiger Großvater
Jahvebärtig
auf braunen Daguerreotypien
Ich seh dein Gesicht
in der schlohweißen Aura
selbstherrlich   streitbar
und die Papiere im Vertiko:
Metzgersrechnungen
Inauguraladressen
Steckbriefe

Deinen massigen Leib
seh ich im Fahndungsbuch
riesiger Hochverräter
displaced person
in Bratenrock und Plastron
schwindsüchtig   schlaflos
die Galle verbrannt
von schweren Zigarren
Salzgurken   Laudanum
und Likör

Ich seh dein Haus
in der rue d'Alliance
Dean Street   Grafton Terrace
riesiger Bourgeois
Haustyrann
in zerschlissnen Pantoffeln:
Ruß und »ökonomische Scheiße«
Pfandleihen »wie gewöhnlich«
Kindersärge
Hintertreppengeschichten

Keine Mitrailleuse
in deiner Prophetenhand:
ich seh sie ruhig

Karl Heinrich Marx

Gigantic grandfather
Jehovah-bearded
on brown daguerrotypes
I see your face
in the snow-white aura
despotic quarrelsome
and your papers in the linen press:
butcher's bills
inaugural addresses
warrants for your arrest

Your massive body
I see in the 'wanted' book
gigantic traitor
displaced person
in tail coat and plastron
consumptive   sleepless
your gall-bladder scorched
by heavy cigars
salted gherkins   laudanum
and liqueur

I see your house
in the rue d'Alliance
Dean Street   Grafton Terrace
gigantic bourgeois
domestic tyrant
in worn-out slippers:
soot and 'economic shit'
pawnshops 'as usual'
children's coffins
backstair calamities

No machine-gun
in your prophet's hand:
I see it peaceably

im British Museum
unter der grünen Lampe
mit fürchterlicher Geduld
dein eigenes Haus zerbrechen
riesiger Gründer
andern Häusern zuliebe
in denen du nimmer erwacht bist

Riesiger Zaddik
Ich seh dich verraten
von deinen Anhängern:
nur deine Feinde
sind dir geblieben:
ich seh dein Gesicht
auf dem letzten Bild
vom April zweiundachtzig:
cine eiserne Maske:
die eiserne Maske der Freiheit

in the British Musuem
under the green lamp
break up your own house
with a terrible patience
gigantic founder
for the sake of other houses
in which you never woke up

Gigantic zaddik
I see you betrayed
by your disciples:
only your enemies
remained what they were:
I see your face
on the last picture
of April eighty-two:
an iron mask:
the iron mask of freedom

Lachesis lapponica

Hier ist es hell, am rostigen Wasser, nirgendwo. Hier,
das sind die Grauweiden, das ist das graue Gras,
das ist der düstere helle Himmel, hier stehe ich.

(*Das ist kein Standpunkt*, sagt der Vogel in meinem Kopf.)

Hier wo ich stehe, das Weiße im Wind sind die Moordaunen,
sieh wie es flimmert. Die leere lautlose Wildnis hier ist die Erde.

(*¡Viva!* ruft der düstere Vogel: (*¡Viva Fidel Castro!*))

Was hat Castro damit zu schaffen! (*Was hast du damit zu schaffen,
mit dem Wollgras, dem Pfeifengras am düsteren Wasser?*)

Nichts, ich habe nichts, Vogel, hörst du? und kein Vogel,
Vogel, kräht nach mir. (*Das ist wahr.*) Laß mich in Ruhe.
Hier kämpfe ich nicht. (Es wird ein Brachvogel sein.)

Dort ist Norden, dort wo es dunkel wird, siehst du,
das Moor wird sehr langsam dunkel. Hier habe ich nichts,
hier habe ich nichts zu tun. Das Weiße im Norden
sind seine Geister, die hellen Geister des Moores.

(*Das ist kein Standpunkt, das sind keine Geister,
das sind Birken*, schreit er, *hier ist nichts los.*)

Das ist gut. Ich kämpfe nicht. Laß mich. Ich warte.

Mit der Zeit, sehr langsam, schält sich die Rinde,
(*ich mache mir nichts daraus*) und das Weiße dort,
das Weiße dort unter dem Weißen, siehst du,
das will ich lesen. (*Und hier*, sagt er, *die genaue Zeit:
dreiundzwanzig Uhr fünfzig.*) Hier, im rostigen Moos.

Lachesis lapponica

Here it is bright, by the rusty water, nowhere. Here,
these are the grey willows, this is the grey grass,
this is the dusky bright sky, here I stand.

(*That is no standpoint*, says the bird in my head.)

Here where I stand, that whiteness in the wind is the moor sedge,
look how it flickers. The silent empty wilderness here is the earth.

(*!Viva!* cries the dusky bird: *!Viva Fidel Castro!*)

What's Castro got to do with it! (*what have you got to do with it,
with the cotton grass, the hair grass by the dusky water?*)

Nothing, I've nothing, bird, do you hear? and no bird,
bird, whistles for me. (*That is true.*) Leave me in peace.
Here I'm not fighting. (It's a curlew, most likely.)

Over there is north, where it's getting dark, you see,
the moor gets dark very slowly. Here I have nothing,
here I have nothing to do. The whiteness up in the north
is the spirits of the north, the moor's bright spirits.

(*That is no standpoint, those are no spirits,
those are birch trees*, it shrieks, *here nothing happens.*)

That's good. I'm not fighting. Leave me. I'm waiting.

In time, very slowly, the bark peels off,
(*it's nothing to me*) and the whiteness there,
the whiteness there under the whiteness, you see,
that I shall read. (*And here*, it says, *the exact time:
twenty-three fifty.*) Here, in the rusty moss.

Ich glaube an Geister (*das gibts nicht!*) leer wild lautlos.
Auch ich bin ein Geist. Auch dieser schreiende Vogel da
in meinem lautlosen Kopf. (*Sag das nicht.*)

Wir blicken beide nach Norden. Mitternacht. (*Am Times Square
stehst du, Toter, ich kenne dich, sehe dich wie du kaufst,
verkaufst und verkauft wirst, du bist es, auf dem Roten Platz,
auf dem Kurfürstendamm, und blickst auf deine rostige Uhr.*)

(Ein Brachvogel wird es sein, oder ein Regenpfeifer.
Sag das nicht, schlag dir das aus dem Kopf.)

Ich schlag dir den Kopf ab, Vogel. (*Es ist dein eigner.
!Viva Fidel! lieber tot als rot! mach mal Pause! Ban the bomb!
Über alles in der Welt!*) Sag das nicht. (*Das alles bist du,*
sagt der Vogel, *stell dir das vor, du bist es gewesen, du bist es.*)

Wie meinst du das? (*Allen Ernstes,* sagt der Vogel und lacht.)
Ein Brachvogel kann nicht lachen. (*Du bist es,* sagt er,
*der lacht. Du wirst es bereuen. Ich weiß, wer du bist,
Totenkopf auf dem Kurfürstendamm.*) Im Moor.

Weiß, düster, grau. Hier sind keine Siege.
Das sind die Moordaunen, das sind die Grauweiden,
das ist der helle Vogel am düsteren Himmel.

Jetzt ist es Mitternacht, jetzt springt die Rinde,
(*die genaue Zeit:*) es ist weiß, (*null Uhr zwei*)
dort im Rauch, wo es dunkel wird, ist es zu lesen,
das unbeschriebene Blatt. Die leere lautlose Wildnis.
Hier ist nichts los. (*Sag das nicht.*) Hier bin ich.
Laß mich. (*Sag das nicht.*) Laß mich allein.

(*Bist du einverstanden, Totenkopf, bist du tot?*
Ist es ein Regenpfeifer? *Wenn du nicht tot bist,
worauf wartest du noch?*) Ich warte. Ich warte.

I believe in spirits (there's no such thing!) empty silent wild.
I too am a spirit. And so is that shrieking bird
in my silent head. (*Don't say that.*)

We both look northward. Midnight. (*On Times Square
you stand, dead man, I know you, I see you buy,
sell and be sold, it is you, on Red Square,
on the Kurfürstendamm, and you look at your rusty watch.*)

(It's a curlew, most likely, or else a peewit.
Don't say that, get it out of your head.)

I'll cut off your head, bird. (*It's your own.
!Viva Fidel! Better dead than red. Have a break! Ban the bomb!
Über alles in der welt!*) Don't say that. (*You are all that,*
says the bird, *imagine, you have been that, you are that.*)

How do you mean? (*In all seriousness*, says the bird and laughs.)
A curlew can't laugh. (*It's yourself*, it says,
*who are laughing. You'll regret it. I know who you are,
death's head on the Kurfürstendamm.*) On the moor.

White, dusky, grey. There are no victories here.
That is the moor sedge, those are the grey willows,
that is the bright bird against the dusky sky.

Now it is midnight, now the bark splits,
(*the exact time:*) it is white, (*zero two minutes*)
there in the mist, where it's getting dark, you can read it,
the blank page. The silent empty wilderness.
Here nothing happens. (*Don't say that.*) Here I am.
Leave me. (*Don't say that.*) Leave me alone.

*Do you agree with me, death's head, and are you dead?
Is it a peewit? If you are not dead
what are you waiting for?* I'm waiting. I'm waiting.

Es ist am äußersten Rand dieser Fläche, Sumpfgras,
Wollgras, Pfeifengras, wo es schon düster ist, Vogel,
(*Wie meinst du das?*) Siehst du? Siehst du die weiße Schrift?

(Feigling, sagt er, *machs gut. Wir sprechen uns noch.*)
Laß mich im Unbeschriebenen. (*Totenkopf.*)
Sieh wie es flimmert. (Und der düstere Vogel
in meinem Kopf sagt zu sich selber: *Er schläft, also
ist er einverstanden.*)
     Aber ich schlafe nicht.

It is on the outermost edge of this plain, marsh grass,
cotton grass, hair grass, where it is dusky already, bird,
(*How do you mean?* Do you see? Do you see the white script?

(*Coward*, it says, *good luck. We shall meet again.*)
Leave me where all is blank. (*Death's head.*)
Look how it flickers. (And the dusky bird
in my head says to itself: *He's asleep, that means
he agrees.*)
             But I am not asleep.

Schattenreich

I

Hier sehe ich noch einen Platz,
einen freien Platz,
hier im Schatten.

II

Dieser Schatten
ist nicht zu verkaufen.

III

Auch das Meer
wirft vielleicht einen Schatten,
auch die Zeit.

IV

Die Kriege der Schatten
sind Spiele:
kein Schatten
steht dem andern im Licht.

V

Wer im Schatten wohnt,
ist schwer zu töten.

VI

Für eine Weile
trete ich aus meinem Schatten,
für eine Weile.

Shadow Realm

I

Here even now I see a place,
a free place,
here in the shadow.

II

This shadow
is not for sale.

III

The sea too
casts a shadow perhaps,
and so does time.

IV

The wars of shadows
are games:
no shadow
stands in another's light.

V

Those who live in the shadow
are difficult to kill.

VI

For a while
I step out of my shadow,
for a while.

VII

Wer das Licht sehen will
wie es ist
muß zurückweichen
in den Schatten.

VIII

Schatten
heller als diese Sonne:
kühler Schatten der Freiheit.

IX

Ganz im Schatten
verschwindet mein Schatten.

X

Im Schatten
ist immer noch Platz.

VII

Those who want to see light
as it is
must retire
into the shadow.

VIII

Shadow
brighter than the sun:
cool shadow of freedom.

IX

Completely in the shadow
my shadow disappears.

X

In the shadow
even now there is room.

POEMS 1955-1970

GEDICHTE 1955-1970

(1971)

Sommergedicht

I

Möglich ist alles
                        daß wir noch nicht tot sind
Eine Tür öffnet sich
                        ein neuer Irrtum
ist mir lieber
                        als alle Gewißheiten
in meinem Mund
                        ein Geschmack nach früher
Kannst du mir helfen?
                        ruft meine Frau
I just hate to be a thing   [Marilyn Monroe
                        aus dem Badezimmer
ein Geruch nach Birken
                        der Wasserhahn rinnt
Spätnachrichten
                        und Vorträge
über Neokapitalismus und Avantgarde

Das ist keine Kunst
                        was noch nicht da ist   [Lao Tse
darauf muß man wirken
                        ein neuer Irrtum
bricht auf
            die Straßen sind leer
ein Mädchen
            in der kürzesten Nacht des Jahres
fais-moi ça
            fais-moi ça
                        auf der Moldau
spielen die Kähne
                        die Lichter sind ausgegangen
in einer alten Gasse
                        die da heißt
                                    Die Neue Welt
brechen

80

Summer Poem

I

Anything is possible
                that we are not dead yet
A door opens
                and I prefer
new errors
                to every certainty
in my mouth
                a taste of earlier times
Can you help me?
                my wife calls out
I just hate to be a thing   [Marilyn Monroe
                        from the bathroom
a smell of birch trees
                        the tap is running
late news
        and radio talks
on neo-capitalism and the avant-garde

No great art in that
        one should work upon that   [Lao-Tse
which does not yet exist
                        a new error
opens up
        the streets are empty
a girl
        in the shortest night of the year
fais-moi ça
                fais-moi ça
                        on the Moldau
the dinghies play the lights
                        have gone out
in an old street
                which there they call:
                        the New World
open

81

alle Arten von Leidenschaften [Wieland

auf

Kannst du mir helfen?

in der weißen Nacht

in der Sauna

in der Dunkelheit

aah!

eine nie zuvor gekannte Empfindung [Wieland

Das Große entsteht aus dem Geringen [Lao Tse
und dazwischen

öffnet sich vielleicht

ein Gedicht

II

Etwas Neues

ein winziger Schrei

bricht auf

etwas Neues

das *alle Springfedern* [Wieland
der Einbildungskraft und des Herzens
zugleich

in einer alten Gasse

spielen macht

im Sonnengeflecht

nach der Liebe

ein winziges Gefühl

von Unsterblichkeit

das sterblichste aller Gefühle

daß wir noch leben

unter soviel toten Leuten

Etwas das früher war

wird kleiner

und kleiner

und ist verschwunden

ein so einziges Schauspiel [Wieland

wohin

überall ist es

überallhin

verschwunden

all the varieties of passion   [Wieland
Can you help me?
                         in the white night
in the sauna
              in the darkness
                         aah!
a sensation never yet known   [Wieland

From little things grows what is great   [Lao Tse
and in between perhaps
                         opens
                              a poem

II

Something new opens
                         a tiny cry
something new
                    since it brings into play   [Wieland
all the springs of imagination
and of the heart
                    in an old street
                              simultaneously
in the solar plexus
                    after love
a tiny sensation
                    of immortality
the most mortal of all sensations
that we are still alive
                         amid so many dead people
Something from earlier times
                              grows smaller
                                   and smaller
and has disappeared
                    a performance so unique   [Wieland
where to
         everywhere it has
                    disappeared
                              to everywhere

Ein Geschmack
          am andern Morgen
nach frischen Erdbeeren
                    die neuen Schlagzeilen
die alte Frage:
          Kannst du mir helfen?
Ich bin kein Kulturinstitut
                    ich leiste
keine Entwicklungshilfe
          Erdbeeren
und Apartheid
          Was tun?   [Lenin
          Eine Ameise
auf der Türschwelle
          schleppt eine tote Fliege fort
und *Womit beginnen?*   [Lenin
          Peking
               Johannesburg
                    überallhin
ist es gleich weit
          und möglich ist alles
Freedom Now
          Johannisfeuer
               Marketing
das ist keine Kunst
          il parlar rotto   [Petrarca
die Tonbänder zwitschern
               dazwischen steigt
in seiner ersten Neuheit   [Wieland
          ein Rezitativ
von Monteverdi auf
          und beweist nichts
Möglich ist es
          daß wir noch leben

Next morning
                a taste
of fresh strawberries
                        the new headlines
the old question:
                Can you help me?
I am no cultural institute
                        I offer
no aid for development
                        strawberries
and apartheid
                What's to be done?   [Lenin
                        An ant
on the threshold
                drags away a dead fly
and *where to begin?*   [Lenin
                Peking
                        Johannesburg
the distance to every place is the same
                                and anything is
                                        possible
Freedom Now
                St John's fire
                        marketing
no great art in that
                il parlar rotto   [Petrarch
the tapes twitter
                in between rises
in its pristine novelty   [Wieland
                        a recitativo
by Monteverdi
                        and proves nothing
It is possible
                that we are still alive

III

Was noch nicht da ist   [Lao Tse
                das ist keine Kunst
meine Welt ist so groß
                in dieser Nacht
wie meine Irrtümer
                kannst du mir helfen?

Ochsenblutrot
                und verschwunden
das hölzerne Haus
                ein Bauernmädchen
aus Karelien
                jetzt ist sie Ansagerin
Spätausgabe
                Tagesschau
                        in der hellsten Nacht
Fernschreiben auf dem Tisch
                        der Mensch   [Norbert Wiener
eine Nachricht
                und überallhin
                        ist es gleich weit

Der chinesische Standpunkt
                        und ein winziger Schrei
öffnet sich
                die *New York Times*
                        das *Pekinger Volksblatt*
in meinen Armen
                dieser Geschmack
                        nach früher
und Birkenlaub
                in der Sauna
                        die Spätnachrichten
aus dem Geringen das Große   [Lao Tse
Mitternacht
                hell genug
                        um Zeitung zu lesen

86

III

That which does not yet exist   [Lao Tse
                              no great art in that
my world is as large
                    in this night
as my errors
              can you help me?

Ox-blood red
              and disappeared
the wooden house
                    a peasant child
from Karelia
              now she's a news reader
late night
          news bulletin
                        in the brightest night
teleprinter on the table
                        man   [Norbert Wiener
is a message
              and the distance to every place
                                        is the same

The Chinese point of view
                        and a tiny cry
opens
      the *New York Times*
                        the *Peking People's Journal*
in my arms
            this taste
                        of earlier times
and birch leaves
                  in the sauna
                        late news
from little things what is great   [Lao Tse
midnight
          bright enough
                        to read a newspaper

87

wir sind die Gegenstände
                    der Gegenstände
unseres Denkens
                    Das Elend der Philosophie   [Marx
und *Womit beginnen?*   [Lenin
                    ich habe das alles gelesen
die Straßen sind leer
                    fais-moi ça
das Mögliche
          öffnet sich
                    die Gräber
unter dem Birkenlaub
                    der frische Mund
der Irrtum
          die helle Nacht

IV

(*Wasserhahn Feuerwerk*
                    Ist das dein Ernst?
Birkenlaub ist passé
                    und *Geschmack nach früher:*
das ist keine Kunst
                    sagte der Kritiker
das geht nicht mehr
                    wirf die Metaphern weg
das ist vorbei

Und ich warf die Metaphern weg
                    ging in die Sauna
und fand
          Birkenlaub
                    und diesen Geschmack
nach früher
          in meinem Mund)

we are the subjects
                    of the subjects of our thinking
the wretchedness of philosophy   [Marx
                    and *where to begin?*   [Lenin

I have read it all
                    the streets are empty
fais-moi ça
                    the possible opens
the graves
                    under the birch leaves
the fresh lips
                    the error
                                        the bright night

IV

(*Water tap fireworks*
                    You can't mean that?
Birch leaves are passé
                    and *a taste of earlier times:*
no great art in that
                    said the critic
                                        you can't get away with
                                                            that now
throw away the metaphors
                    they're a thing of the past

And I threw away the metaphors
and went to the sauna
                    and found
birch leaves
                    and this taste of earlier times
in my mouth)

V

Schlafen wir also
                  leicht und irrtümlich
und es wecke uns keiner
                      und sage:
Kannst du mir helfen?
                      Hier in diesem Hotel
wird heute nacht
                  niemand erschossen
der Wasserhahn rinnt
                      woanders
der Start
        in die leere Zukunft
Glorien
        Brander
                  und Satelliten
                              aah!
ein so wunderbares Schauspiel   [Wieland

Auch ich bin gefahren
                      in *das*   [Lao Tse
was noch nicht da ist
                      durchs Pentagon
auf einem Tretroller
                  in Tränen
eine nie zuvor gekannte Empfindung   [Wieland

Der Touristenkurs hier
                  ist günstig
für den Irrtum
            woanders
                      finden die Kriege statt
aber überallhin
            ist es gleich weit
für den geringen Schrei
                  die Spätnachrichten
Feuerräder
        Schwärmer
                  und Sonnen

V

Let us sleep then
     lightly erroneously
and let no one awaken us
      saying:
Can you help me?
     Here in this hotel
tonight
   no one is being shot
the tap is running
     elsewhere
the take-off
    into an empty future
squibs
  golden rain
    and satellites
      aah!
a performance so wonderful   [Wieland

I too have travelled
     to *that*   [Lao Tse
which does not yet exist
     through the pentagon
on a treadle scooter
    in tears
a sensation never yet known   [Wieland

Here the tourist rate of exchange
      is favourable
to error
  elsewhere
    the wars take place
but the distance
    to every place is the same
for the little cry
    the late news
tourbillions
   nebulae
    and rockets

und das Mögliche
          hat einen leichten Schlaf
                              neben mir
In den alten Augen
                    eines alten Freundes
aus Tilsit
          die nicht viel von der Zukunft halten
lese ich
          das Geringe   [Lao Tse
                    aus dem das Große entsteht
vielleicht
          in der Mitternacht
                              sitzen wir
Johannes Bobrowski und ich
                              betrunken
der Wasserhahn rinnt
                    il subito silenzio   [Petrarca
in der Sauna
          Kannst du mir helfen?

VI

Ich habe soviel
                tote Leute
                              gesehen
und doch ist noch nichts entschieden
in diesem Sommer
                    mitten im Ausverkauf
Erdbeeren
          Umsätze
                    und dieser Geschmack
nach Verschwundenheit
                    ist überall
und nach Birkenlaub
Gewisse Sicherheitsfunktionen   [Deutsche Bank AG
                    beim Start
ein kleiner Schrei
          gewichtlos
                    überall

and the possible
           sleeps lightly
                      at my side
In the ancient eyes
              of an old friend
from Tilsit
that don't think much of the future
                        I read
the little things   [Lao Tse
          from which *grows what is great*
maybe
      at midnight
           we sit
Johannes Bobrowski and I
                drunk
the tap is running
           il subito silenzio   [Petrarch
in the sauna
         Can you help me?

VI

I have seen
        so many
                dead people
and yet nothing has been decided
this summer
            at the height of the sales
strawberries
          turnovers
               and this taste
of something disappeared
                  is everywhere
and of birch leaves
certain safety measures   [Deutsche Bank AG
            at the take-off
a little cry
         weightless
            everywhere

ist der Mittelpunkt
          und ein neuer Irrtum
steigt feurig auf
          das Mögliche ist
eine Exponentialfunktion
               aller Arten von Leidenschaften   [Wieland
die das Gefühl des Erhabenen
               bei der maschinellen   [Deutsche Bank AG
Bearbeitung der Umsätze
                    in der Seele   [Wieland
entzünden kann
          und öffnet sich
               über den Wolken
                    aah!

schwebt
     und verschwindet
               hoch
in seiner ersten Neuheit   [Wieland
               über den leeren Straßen
ein Fenster
          öffnet sich
               jemand weint
Über die Behandlung der Widersprüche im Volk   [Mao Tse-Tung

Das Mögliche
          genügt nicht
               Was noch nicht da ist   [Lao Tse
beweist nichts
          die Lichter
               über der Moldau
i lunghi pianti   [Petrarca
          die Lichter
               sind ausgegangen

is the centre
            and a new error
rises fiery
            arc of the possible
exponential function
                        of all the varieties of passion   [Wieland
which can kindle
                        in the mechanical   [Deutsche Bank AG
calculation of turnovers
                        a sense of the sublime   [Wieland
in the soul
            and opens
                        above the clouds
                                    aah!
hovers
        and disappears
                        high up
in its pristine novelty
                        above the empty streets   [Wieland
a window
            opens
                        somebody weeps
about the correct handling of contradictions among the people
                                                [Mao Tse Tung
The possible
            is not enough
                        That which does not yet exist   [Lao Tse
proves nothing
                        the lights
                                    over the Moldau
i lunghi pianti   [Petrarch
                        the lights
                                    have gone out

VII

Womit beginnen [Lenin
      in dieser flüchtigen Nacht
am Päijänne-See
        an der Moldau
           oder woanders
mein erbitterter Freund
         betrachtet die Socken
der vorübergehenden
         der *verratenen* [Trockij
Revolution
      wer stopft sie
        die *Dialektik des Konkreten* [Karel Kosik
wer flickt sie
       vorübergehende Fehler
und *gewisse Sicherheitsfunktionen* [Deutsche Bank AG
           bei der maschinellen
Bearbeitung
      der Widersprüche im Volk [Mao Tse-Tung

Ein neuer Irrtum
       das ist keine Kunst
ein Feuerwerk
      bricht auf
        über dem Fluß
Spiralen
    Glorien
      Sonden
e'l brevissimo riso [Petrarca
      leuchtet
        steigt
aah!
  Gulasch umd Kommunismus [Chruscev
        und meine Frau
der Standpunkt der Dritten Welt
        Kannst du
mir helfen?
    Ein Gedicht ist kein Brot

VII

Where to begin   [Lenin
            in this brief night
by the Päijänne lake
            by the Moldau
                        or elsewhere
my embittered friend
            looks at the socks
of those who pass by
            of the betrayed   [Trotski
revolution
        who will mend them
            the *dialectic of the concrete*   [Karel Kosik
who will patch them
                    passing errors
and *certain safety measures*   [Deutsche Bank AG
                    in the mechanical
calculation
            of *contradictions among the people*   [Mao Tse Tung

A new error
            no great art in that
a firework
        opens
            above the river
girandoles
        squibs
                tourbillons
e'l brevissimo riso   [Petrarch
            shines
                    rises
aah!
    goulash and communism   [Khrushchev
                    and my wife
the point of view of the third world
                        Can you
help me?
        a poem is not bread

97

und meine Frau
            geht langsam
                        über die Brücke
und singt vor sich hin
                     etwas Geringes
das fliegen kann
              und verschwindet
                       in dem
was noch nicht da ist
           so hell ist die Nacht

VIII

Ein Schritt vorwärts   [Lenin
         zwei Schritte zurück
im schattenbefleckten Laub
               vor der Orangerie
dein Gesicht in Tränen
              e i lunghi pianti   [Petrarca
I just hate to be a thing   [Marilyn Monroe

Tarifverhandlungen
           Weizenpreise
                  Dantestudien
ich habe das alles gelesen
             das ist keine Kunst

Überallhin
        fallen die alten Schatten
an den Rändern
              brechen neue Irrtümer auf
rascheln
       in unsern Mündern
               wie Birkenlaub
dieser Geschmack
        in der Nacht
ein Fenster öffnet sich
          ein Gedicht

and my wife
                walks slowly
                                over the bridge
and sings to herself
                        something small
that can fly
                and disappears
                                in that
which does not yet exist
                        so bright the night is

VIII

A step forward   [Lenin
                two steps back
in shade-mottled leafage
                                in front of the orangerie
your face bathed in tears
                                e i lunghi pianti   [Petrarch
I just hate to be a thing   [Marilyn Monroe

Tariff negotiations
                        wheat prices
                                        Dante studies
I have read it all
                no great art in that

Everywhere
                the old shadows fall
at the edges
                new errors open
rustle
        in our mouths
                                like birch leaves
this taste
        in the night
a window opens
                        a poem

Über den Widerspruch   [Mao Tse-Tung
        und der jähe Start
            aah!

ein so großes   [Wieland
    so wunderbares
        so schauerliches
so einziges Schauspiel
        der Start in *das*   [Lao Tse
was noch nicht da ist
        überall
            gleichzeitig
spielen die Rentner Skat
        in Neukölln
ein Feuerwerk
        auf der Moldau
            auf dem Bildschirm
auf dem Päijänne-See
        die Kähne
            spielen
alle Springfedern der Einbildungskraft   [Wieland
beim Start
        in das Reich der Freiheit
vor der Sauna
        Johannisfeuer
            und frische Erdbeeren
auf dem Tisch
        in der kürzesten Nacht
            dieses Jahres (1964)
an den Rändern
        rascheln
            unsere Münder
wie Reispapier
        Nachrichten
            Ratschläge   [Lenin
eines Außenstehenden
        (Finnland 1917)
und ein Irrtum schreit
        fais-moi ça

about contradiction [Mao Tse-Tung
      and the sudden take-off
              aah!
a performance [Wieland
     so wonderful
        so uncanny
so unique
     the take-off into that
which does not yet exist [Lao Tse
       everywhere
         at the same time
the rentiers are playing whist
         in Neukölln
a firework display
      on the Moldau
         on the television screen
on the Päijänne lake
      the dinghies
        play
all the springs of the imagination [Wieland
at the take-off into
the realm of freedom
       in front of the sauna
St John's fire
     and fresh strawberries
on the table
     in the shortest night
       of this year (1964)
at the edges
    rustle
     our mouths
like rice paper
    news
      an outsider's [Lenin
advice
   (Finland 1917)
and an error screams
     fais-moi ça

ein so wunderbares Schauspiel   [Wieland
muß in seiner ersten Neuheit
einen Grad von Entzücken hervorbringen

Ein Gedicht bricht auf
                    e'l parlar rotto   [Petrarca
und verschwindet
          e'l subito silenzio
und alles ist möglich
               e'l brevissimo riso
und steigt
     e i lunghi pianti
und verschwindet
                    und ist verschwunden

a performance so wonderful   [Wieland
in its pristine novelty must produce
such a degree of rapture

A poem opens
            e'l parlar rotto   [Petrarch
and disappears
            e'l subito silenzio
and anything is possible
                        e'l brevissimo riso
and rises
        e i lunghi pianti
and disappears
                and has disappeared

Note on *Summer Poem*

Summer Poem was written in 1964. Its occasion was autobiographical: two journeys, one to Prague and one to Finland. The two thematic pivots of the poem are political and erotic experience.

Its formal principle is that of openness. One can regard poems either as closed and sealed, as impermeable structures, or as net-like constructions with which new experiences can be caught again and again – even when the writing of the text is finished. This intention determines the technique and structure of *Summer Poem.*

The geographical centres of the poem, Prague and Lake Päijänne in Finland, are not presented as landscape pictures, but are stations in a comprehensive network of communications in which 'all distances are the same'. That is why the exploited countries of the world are included, and a news item from Peking is as real in the Finnish sauna as in New York.

This nexus is caught in flight and acceleration, in the twittering of sound tapes, in the *parlar rotto*, the broken speech of our media, in the flood of distorted information from Dante studies to the *Peking People's Journal*. That is the point of the quotations. Thus the prose text by Wieland is taken from a description of early attempts to fly in the eighteenth century (*The Aeronauts*, 1778).

Mobility is not confined to the dimension of space, but extends to time. With the taste of a vanished past in our mouths (the Italian phrases are from Petrarch's *Trionfo d'Amore*) we take off into a future to which our imagination seems not to be equal. The demographic and technological curves rise exponentially. 'That which does not yet exist' moves even those who are not aware of it. At the same time the thing that used to be called art enters a kind of twilight. 'There's no art in that' – the traditional objection of a bourgeois aesthetic against every innovation becomes baseless: only the censor knows what is art.

This twilight, the 'bright night' of the northern summer, is the horizon of the poem, as it were. The fireworks, a technological celebration, from harmless playthings to the rockets of the astronauts and of nuclear strategy, have become the St John's fire of our summer. (Girandoles, tourbillons, etc. are terms from pyrotechnics.) Our rapid movements are a flight from something, but also an advance towards something. Literary language has a tendency to tie down anything that can be said. This text opposes the tendency by breaking up sentences. That is why the poem is dominated by a kind of syntax which classical grammar calls *apo koinou*: four sentence parts are related in such a way that the sentence can be read in several different ways.

The repetitions in the poem serve to subject the experiences dealt with to doubt, to contradiction, to questioning. Thus the phrase 'Can you help me?' refers to something different each time it occurs, and the sentimental phrases from Wieland function as irony in one place, as solemn paraphrase in another. Permutation, collage, simultaneity are not new devices, and mere virtuosity bores us. A poem intended to be, and to remain, open must make the critique of itself as part of its movement. It participates in the twilight of which it speaks and must finally vanish in it if it is not to give itself the lie.

HANS MAGNUS ENZENSBERGER
translated by Michael Hamburger

Die Freude

Sie will nicht daß ich von ihr rede
Sie steht nicht auf dem Papier
Sie duldet keinen Propheten

Sie ist eine Fremde
doch ich kenne sie
Ich kenne sie gut

Sie wirft alles um was fest steht
Sie lügt nicht
Sie meutert

Sie allein rechtfertigt mich
Sie ist meine Vernunft
Sie gehört mir nicht

Sie ist fremd und beharrlich
Ich verberge sie
wie eine Schande

Sie ist flüchtig
Niemand kann sie teilen
Niemand kann sie für sich behalten

Ich behalte nichts
Ich teile alles mit ihr
Sie wird fortgehen

Ein anderer wird sie verbergen
auf ihrer siegreichen Flucht
durch die sehr lange Nacht

Joy

She does not want me to speak of her
She won't be put down on paper
She can't stand prophets

She is a stranger
but I know her
I know her well

She will overthrow all that is settled and fast
She will not lie
She will riot

By her alone I am justified
She is my reason, my reason of state
She does not belong to me

She is strange and headstrong
I harbour, I hide her
like a disgrace

She is a fugitive
not to be shared with others
not to be kept for yourself

I keep nothing from her
I share with her all I have
She will leave me

Others will harbour her
on her long flight to victory
and hide her by night

Gedicht über die Zukunft, November 1964

Zwei Männer kommen auf einem Traktor
(Chou En-Lai ist in Moskau)
Zwei Männer in steingrauen Kitteln
(Nobelpreisträger im Frack)
Zwei Männer mit dünnen Stecken
(Goldmedaillen aus Tokio)
am Straßenrand zwischen gelben Blättern
(die toten Guerrilleros von Vietnam)

Zwischen die lehmgelben Blätter
stecken zwei Männer in grauen Kitteln
am Straßenrand dünne Stöcke
alle fünfzig Schritt einen links einen rechts
dunkle Stöcke im hellen November
(Chou En-Lai ist in Moskau)

Zwei Männer in grauen Kitteln
riechen im flachen Novemberlicht
den Schnee der zudecken wird
Blätter und Männer

bis kein Weg mehr zu sehen ist
nur noch alle fünfzig Schritt
ein dünner Stock links
ein dünner Stock rechts
damit der Schneepflug
wo kein Weg mehr zu sehen ist
einen Weg finde

Poem about the Future

Two men appear on a tractor
(Chou En-Lai is in Moscow)
Two men in stone-grey overalls
(Nobel Prize winners in evening dress)
Two men with slender sticks
(gold medals from Tokyo)
at the wayside amid yellow leaves
(the dead guerillas of Vietnam)

Among the clay-yellow leaves
two men in grey overalls
put up slender sticks at the wayside
one left one right every fifty paces
dark sticks in bright November
(Chou En-Lai is in Moscow)

Two men in grey overalls
scent in the shallow November light
the snow that will cover
leaves and men

till no way is to be seen
only at every fiftieth pace
a slender stick on the left
a slender stick on the right
so that the snow-plough
will find a way
where no way is to be seen

Lied von denen auf die alles zutrifft und die alles schon wissen

Daß etwas getan werden muß und zwar sofort
das wissen wir schon
daß es aber noch zu früh ist um etwas zu tun
daß es aber zu spät ist um noch etwas zu tun
das wissen wir schon

und daß es uns gut geht
und daß es so weiter geht
und daß es keinen Zweck hat
das wissen wir schon

und daß wir schuld sind
und daß wir nichts dafür können daß wir schuld sind
und daß wir daran schuld sind daß wir nichts dafür können
und daß es uns reicht
das wissen wir schon

und daß es vielleicht besser wäre die Fresse zu halten
und daß wir die Fresse nicht halten werden
das wissen wir schon
das wissen wir schon

und daß wir niemand helfen können
und daß uns niemand helfen kann
das wissen wir schon

und daß wir begabt sind
und daß wir die Wahl haben zwischen nichts und wieder nichts
und daß wir dieses Problem gründlich analysieren müssen
und daß wir zwei Stück Zucker in den Tee tun
das wissen wir schon

und daß wir gegen die Unterdrückung sind
und daß die Zigaretten teurer werden
das wissen wir schon

Song for Those Who Know

Something must be done right away
that much we know
but of course it's too soon to act
but of course it's too late in the day
oh we know

we know that we're really rather well off
and that we'll go on like this
and that it's not much use anyway
oh we know

we know that we are to blame
and that it's not our fault if we are to blame
and that we're to blame for the fact that it's not our fault
and that we're fed up with it
oh we know

and that maybe it would be a good idea to keep our mouths shut
and that we won't keep our mouths shut all the same
oh we know
oh we know

and we also know that we can't help anybody really
and that nobody really can help us
oh we know

and that we're extremely gifted and brilliant
and free to choose between nothing and naught
and that we must analyse this problem very carefully
and that we take two lumps of sugar in our tea
oh we know

we know all about oppression
and that we are very much against it
and that cigarettes have gone up again

und daß wir es jedesmal kommen sehen
und daß wir jedesmal recht behalten werden
und daß daraus nichts folgt
das wissen wir schon

und daß das alles wahr ist
das wissen wir schon

und daß das alles gelogen ist
das wissen wir schon

und daß das alles ist
das wissen wir schon

und daß Überstehn nicht alles ist sondern gar nichts
das wissen wir schon

und daß wir es überstehn
das wissen wir schon

und daß das alles nicht neu ist
und daß das Leben schön ist
das wissen wir schon
das wissen wir schon
das wissen wir schon

und daß wir das schon wissen
das wissen wir schon

oh we know
we know very well that the nation is heading for real trouble
and that our forecasts have usually been dead right
and that they are not of any use
and that all this is just talk
oh we know

that it's just not good enough to live things down
and that we are going to live them down all the same
oh we know oh we know

that there is nothing new in all this
and that life is wonderful
and that's all there is to it
oh we know all this perfectly well

and that we know all this perfectly well
oh we know that too
oh we know it
oh we know

Rondeau

Reden ist leicht.

Aber Wörter kann man nicht essen.
Also backe Brot.
Brot backen ist schwer.
Also werde Bäcker.

Aber in einem Brot kann man nicht wohnen.
Also bau Häuser.
Häuser bauen ist schwer.
Also werde Maurer.

Aber auf einen Berg kann man kein Haus bauen.
Also versetze den Berg.
Berge versetzen ist schwer.
Also werde Prophet.

Aber Gedanken kann man nicht hören.
Also rede.
Reden ist schwer.
Also werde was du bist

und murmle weiter vor dich hin,
unnützes Geschöpf.

Rondeau

It's easy to talk.

But you can't eat words.
So bake bread.
It's hard to bake bread.
So become a baker.

But you can't live in a loaf.
So build houses.
It's hard to build houses.
So become a bricklayer.

But you can't build a house on a mountain.
So move the mountain.
It's hard to move mountains.
So become a prophet.

But you can't hear thoughts.
So talk.
It's hard to talk.
So become what you are

and keep on muttering to yourself,
useless creature.

Die Macht der Gewohnheit

Gewohnheit macht den Fehler schön.

CHRISTIAN FÜRCHTEGOTT GELLERT

I

Gewöhnliche Menschen haben für gewöhnlich
für gewöhnliche Menschen nichts übrig.
Und umgekehrt.
Gewöhnliche Menschen finden es ungewöhnlich,
daß man sie ungewöhnlich findet.
Schon sind sie keine gewöhnlichen Menschen mehr.
Und umgekehrt.

II

Daß man sich an alles gewöhnt,
daran gewöhnt man sich.
Man nennt das gewöhnlich
einen Lernprozeß.

III

Es ist schmerzlich,
wenn der gewohnte Schmerz ausbleibt.
Wie müde ist das aufgeweckte Gemüt
seiner Aufgewecktheit!
Der einfache Mensch da z. B. findet es schwierig,
ein einfacher Mensch zu sein,
während jene komplexe Persönlichkeit
ihre Schwierigkeiten herleiert
wie die Betschwester den Rosenkranz.
Überall diese ewigen Anfänger,
die längst am Ende sind.
Auch der Haß ist eine liebe Gewohnheit.

The Force of Habit

Habit makes beautiful the fault.

CHRISTIAN FÜRCHTEGOTT GELLERT

I

Ordinary people ordinarily do not care
for ordinary people.
And vice versa.
Ordinary people find it extraordinary
that people find them extraordinary.
At once they have ceased to be ordinary.
And vice versa.

II

That one gets used to everything –
one gets used to that.
The usual name for it is
a learning process.

III

It is painful
when the habitual pain does not present itself.
How tired the lively mind
is of its liveliness!
The simple person there for instance finds it complicated
to be a simple person,
while that complex character
rattles off his complexity
as nuns do their rosaries.
All these eternal beginners
who long ago reached the end.
Hatred, too, is a precious habit.

IV

Das noch nie Dagewesene
sind wir gewohnt.
Das noch nie Dagewesene
ist ein Gewohnheitsrecht.
Ein Gewohnheitstier
trifft an der gewohnten Ecke
einen Gewohnheitsverbrecher.
Eine unerhörte Begebenheit.
Die gewöhnliche Scheiße.
Die Klassiker waren gewöhnt,
Novellen daraus zu machen.

V

Sanft ruhet die Gewohnheit der Macht
auf der Macht der Gewohnheit.

IV

The utterly unprecedented –
we are used to that.
The utterly unprecedented
is our habitual right.
A creature of habit
at the usual corner meets
an habitual criminal.
An unheard-of occurrence.
The usual shit.
Our 'classics' were in the habit
of turning it into stories.

V

Untroubled the habit of force reposes
on the force of habit.

Hommage à Gödel

Münchhausens Theorem, Pferd, Sumpf und Schopf,
ist bezaubernd, aber vergiß nicht:
Münchhausen war ein Lügner.

Gödels Theorem wirkt auf den ersten Blick
etwas unscheinbar, doch bedenk:
Gödel hat recht.

»In jedem genügend reichhaltigen System
lassen sich Sätze formulieren,
die innerhalb des Systems
weder beweis- noch widerlegbar sind,
es sei denn das System
wäre selber inkonsistent.«

Du kannst deine eigene Sprache
in deiner eigenen Sprache beschreiben:
aber nicht ganz.
Du kannst dein eignes Gehirn
mit deinem eignen Gehirn erforschen:
aber nicht ganz.
Usw.

Um sich zu rechtfertigen
muß jedes denkbare System
sich transzendieren,
d.h. zerstören.

»Genügend reichhaltig« oder nicht:
Widerspruchsfreiheit
ist eine Mangelerscheinung
oder ein Widerspruch.

(Gewißheit = Inkonsistenz.)

Homage to Gödel

'Pull yourself out of the mire
by your own hair': Münchausen's theorem
is charming, but do not forget:
the Baron was a great liar.

Gödel's theorem may seem, at first sight,
rather nondescript,
but please keep in mind:
Gödel is right.

'In any sufficiently rich system
statements are possible
which can neither be proved
nor refuted within the system,
unless the system itself
is inconsistent.'

You can describe your own language
in your own language:
but not quite.
You can investigate your own brain
by means of your own brain:
but not quite.
Etc.

In order to be vindicated
any conceivable system
must transcend, and that means,
destroy itself.

'Sufficiently rich' or not:
Freedom from contradiction
is either a deficiency symptom,
or it amounts to a contradiction.

(Certainty = Inconsistency.)

Jeder denkbare Reiter,
also auch Münchhausen,
also auch du bist ein Subsystem
eines genügend reichhaltigen Sumpfes.

Und ein Subsystem dieses Subsystems
ist der eigene Schopf,
dieses Hebezeug
für Reformisten und Lügner.

In jedem genügend reichhaltigen System,
also auch in diesem Sumpf hier,
lassen sich Sätze formulieren,
die innerhalb des Systems
weder beweis- noch widerlegbar sind.

Diese Sätze nimm in die Hand
und zieh!

Any conceivable horseman,
including Münchausen,
including yourself, is a subsystem
of a sufficiently rich mire.

And a subsystem of this subsystem
is your own hair,
favourite tackle
of reformists and liars.

In any sufficiently rich system
including the present mire
statements are possible
which can neither be proved
nor refuted within the system.

Those are the statements
to grasp, and pull!

Wunschkonzert

Samad sagt Gib mir einen Fladen Brot
Frl. Brockmann sucht eine gemütliche kleine Komfortwohnung
   nicht zu teuer mit Kochnische und Besenkammer
Veronique sehnt sich nach der Weltrevolution
Dr Luhmann möchte unbedingt mit seiner Mamma schlafen
Uwe Köpke träumt von einem Kabinettstück Thurn und Taxis
   sieben Silbergroschen hellblau ungezähnt
Simone weiß ganz genau was sie will Berühmt sein Einfach berühmt
   sein ganz egal wofür und um welchen Preis
Wenn es nach Konrad ginge bliebe er einfach im Bett liegen
Mrs Woods möchte andauernd gefesselt und vergewaltigt werden
   aber nur von hinten und nur von einem Gentleman
Guido Ronconis einziger Wunsch ist die unio mystica
Fred Podritzke schlüge am liebsten mit einem Gasrohr auf all diese
   Spinner ein bis sich keiner mehr rührte
Wenn er jetzt nicht sofort sein Sahneschnitzel mit Gurkensalat
   bekommt wird Karel aber durchdrehen
Was Buck braucht ist ein Flash und sonst nichts

Und Friede auf Erden und ein Heringsbrötchen und den herr-
   schaftsfreien Diskurs und ein Baby und eine Million steuerfrei
   und ein Stöhnen das in die bekannten kleinen atemlosen Schreie
   übergeht und einen Pudel aus Plüsch und Freiheit für alle und
   Kopf ab und daß uns die ausgefallenen Haare wieder nachwach-
   sen über Nacht

Concert of Wishes

Sanad says: Give me my daily pita

Fräulein Brockmann looks for a comfortable little flat not too expensive with a cooking recess and a broom cupboard

Véronique longs for world revolution

Dr Luhmann desperately needs to sleep with his mum

Uwe Köpke dreams of a perfect specimen of Thurn and Taxis seven silbergroschen pale blue imperforated

Simone knows exactly what she wants: to be famous Simply famous no matter what for or at what price

If Konrad had his way he'd simply lie in bed for ever

Mrs Woods would like to be tied up and raped quite regularly but only from behind and by a gentleman

Guido Ronconi's only desire is the unio mystica

Fred Podritzke would love to work over all those crackpot lefties with a length of gas piping until not one of them so much as twitches

If someone doesn't give him his steak and chips this minute Karel will blow his top

What Buck needs is a flash and nothing else

And peace on earth and a ham sandwich and the uncensored dialogue and a baby and a million free of tax and a moaning that gives way to the familiar little breathless shrieks and a plush poodle and freedom for all and off with his head and that the hair we have lost will grow again overnight

THE SINKING OF THE TITANIC
DER UNTERGANG DER TITANIC
(1978)

Apokalypse. Umbrisch, etwa 1490

Er ist nicht mehr der Jüngste, er seufzt,
er holt eine große Leinwand hervor, er grübelt,
verhandelt lang und zäh mit dem Besteller,
einem geizigen Karmeliter aus den Abruzzen,
Prior oder Kapitular. Schon wird es Winter,
die Fingergelenke knacken, das Reisig
knackt im Kamin. Er seufzt, grundiert,
läßt trocknen, grundiert ein andermal,
kritzelt, ungeduldig, auf kleine Kartons
seine Figuren, schemenhaft, hebt sie mit Deckweiß.
Er zaudert, reibt Farben an, vertrödelt
mehrere Wochen. Dann, eines Tages, es ist
unterdessen Aschermittwoch geworden
oder Mariä Lichtmeß, taucht er, in aller Frühe,
den Pinsel in die gebrannte Umbra und malt:
Das wird ein dunkles Bild. Wie fängt man es an,
den Weltuntergang zu malen? Die Feuersbrünste,
die entflohenen Inseln, die Blitze, die sonderbar
allmählich einstürzenden Mauern, Zinnen und Türme:
technische Fragen, Kompositionsprobleme.
Die ganze Welt zu zerstören macht viel Arbeit.
Besonders schwer sind die Geräusche zu malen,
das Zerreißen des Vorhangs im Tempel,
die brüllenden Tiere, der Donner. Alles
soll nämlich zerreißen, zerrissen werden,
nur nicht die Leinwand. Und der Termin
steht fest: Allerspätestens Allerseelen.
Bis dahin muß, im Hintergrund, das wütende Meer
lasiert werden, tausendfach, mit grünen,
schaumigen Lichtern, durchbohrt von Masten,
lotrecht in die Tiefe schießenden Schiffen,
Wracks, während draußen, mitten im Juli,
kein Hund sich regt auf dem staubigen Platz.
Der Maler ist ganz allein in der Stadt geblieben,
verlassen von Frauen, Schülern, Gesinde.
Müde scheint er, wer hätte das gedacht,

Apocalypse. Umbrian Master, about 1490

He is not as young as he used to be. With a groan
he chooses a sizeable canvas. He broods on it.
He wastes his time haggling about his commission
with a mean Carmelite monk from the Abruzzi,
prior, or canon, or whatnot. It is winter now.
His finger joints start cracking like the brushwood
in the fireplace. With a groan he will ground
the canvas, let it dry, ground it once more,
will scrawl his figures, impatiently, ghostlike,
on small cartoons, and set them off with white lead.
He temporises and idles away a few weeks,
rubbing down his colours. But at long last –
Ash Wednesday has gone by, and Candlemas –
early one morning he dips his brush in burnt umber
and starts painting. This will be a gloomy picture.
How do you go about painting Doom? The conflagrations,
the vanishing islands, the lightning, the walls
and towers and pinnacles crumbling ever so slowly:
nice points of technique, problems of composition.
Destroying the world is a difficult exercise.
Hardest to paint are the sounds – for example
the temple veil being rent asunder, the beasts
roaring, and the thunderclaps. Everything, you see,
is to be rent asunder and torn to pieces,
except the canvas. And there can be no doubt
about the appointed time: by All Souls' Day
the frantic sea in the background must be coated
over and over again with a thousand layers
of transparency, with foamy green lights,
pierced by mastheads, by ships reeling, plunging down,
by wrecks, while outside, in mid-July,
not a dog will stir on the dust-covered square.
The women have left, the servants, the disciples.
In the forlorn town only the Master remains.
He looks tired. Who would have thought that he, of all people,
would look dead tired? Ochre – everything seems ochre now,

sterbensmüde. Alles ist ocker, schattenlos,
steht starr da, hält still in einer Art
böser Ewigkeit; nur das Bild nicht. Das Bild
nimmt zu, verdunkelt sich langsam, füllt sich
mit Schatten, stahlblau, erdgrau, trübviolett,
caput mortuum; füllt sich mit Teufeln, Reitern,
Gemetzeln; bis daß der Weltuntergang
glücklich vollendet ist, und der Maler
erleichtert, für einen kurzen Augenblick;
unsinnig heiter, wie ein Kind,
als wär ihm das Leben geschenkt,
lädt er, noch für denselben Abend,
Frauen, Kinder, Freunde und Feinde
zum Wein, zu frischen Trüffeln und Bekassinen,
während draußen der erste Herbstregen rauscht.

shadowless, standing still, transfixed in a kind
of evil eternity, except the picture. It grows
and darkens slowly, absorbing shadows,
steel-blue; livid, dull violet, caput mortuum,
absorbing demons and horsemen and massacres,
until Doom is happily consummated and the artist,
for a brief moment, is, like a child, unmindfully merry,
as if his life had been spared, and in his relief
on this very night he asks his friends to a feast
and treats them to truffles, to grouse and old wine,
with the season's first rainstorm pounding away at the shutters.

Verlustanzeige

Die Haare verlieren, die Nerven,
versteht ihr, die kostbare Zeit,
auf verlorenem Posten an Höhe
verlieren, an Glanz, ich bedaure,
macht nichts, nach Punkten,
unterbrecht mich nicht, Blut
verlieren, Vater und Mutter,
das in Heidelberg verlorene Herz,
ohne mit der Wimper zu zucken,
noch einmal verlieren, den Reiz
der Neuheit, Schwamm drüber,
die bürgerlichen Ehrenrechte, aha,
den Kopf, in Gottesnamen, den Kopf,
wenn es unbedingt sein muß,
das verlorene Paradies, meinetwegen,
den Arbeitsplatz, den Verlorenen Sohn,
das Gesicht, auch das noch,
einen Backenzahn, zwei Weltkriege,
drei Kilo Übergewicht verlieren,
verlieren, immer nur verlieren, auch
die längst verlorenen Illusionen,
na wenn schon, kein Wort
über die verlorene Liebesmüh,
aber woher denn, das Augenlicht
aus den Augen, die Unschuld
verlieren, schade, den Hausschlüssel,
schade, sich, gedankenverloren,
in der Menge verlieren,
unterbrecht mich nicht,
den Verstand, den letzten Heller,
sei's drum, gleich bin ich fertig,
die Fassung, Hopfen und Malz,
alles auf einmal verlieren,
wehe, sogar den Faden,
den Führerschein, und die Lust.

Notice of Loss

To lose your hair, to lose your temper,
if you see what I mean, your precious time,
to fight a losing battle,
losing height and lustre, sorry,
never mind, to lose on points,
let me bloody well finish,
to lose blood, father and mother,
to lose your heart, lost long ago
in Heidelberg, all over again,
without batting an eye, the charm
of novelty, forget it, to lose
civic rights, I get the message,
to lose your head, by all means,
if it can't be helped,
to lose Paradise Lost, what next,
your job, the Prodigal Son,
to lose face, good riddance,
two World Wars, one molar,
seven pounds of overweight,
to lose, lose, and lose again, even
your illusions long ago lost,
so what, let us not waste another word
on love's labour lost, I should say not,
to lose sight of your lost sight,
your virginity, what a pity, your keys,
what a pity, to get lost in the crowd,
lost in thoughts, let me finish,
to lose your mind, your last penny,
no matter, I'll be through in a moment,
your lost causes, all sense of shame,
everything, blow by blow,
alas, even the thread of your story,
your driver's licence, your soul.

Abendmahl. Venezianisch, 16 Jahrhundert

I

Als ich mein *Letztes Abendmahl* beendet hatte,
fünfeinhalb mal knapp dreizehn Meter,
eine Heidenarbeit, aber ganz gut bezahlt,
kamen die üblichen Fragen.
Was haben diese Ausländer zu bedeuten
mit ihren Hellebarden? Wie Ketzer
sind sie gekleidet, oder wie Deutsche.
Finden Sie es wohl schicklich,
dem Heiligen Lukas
einen Zahnstocher in die Hand zu geben?
Wer hat Sie dazu angestiftet,
Mohren, Säufer und Clowns
an den Tisch Unseres Herrn zu laden?
Was soll dieser Zwerg mit dem Papagei,
was soll der schnüffelnde Hund,
und warum blutet der Mameluck aus der Nase?
Meine Herrn, sprach ich, dies alles
habe ich frei erfunden zu meinem Vergnügen.
Aber die Sieben Richter der Heiligen Inquisition
raschelten mit ihren roten Roben
und murmelten: Überzeugt uns nicht.

II

Oh, ich habe bessere Bilder gemalt;
aber jener Himmel zeigt Farben,
die ihr auf keinem Himmel findet,
der nicht von mir gemalt ist;
und es gefallen mir diese Köche
mit ihren riesigen Metzgersmessern,
diese Leute mit Diademen, mit Reiherbüschen,
pelzverbrämten, gezaddelten Hauben
und perlenbestickten Turbanen;
auch jene Vermummten gehören dazu,
die auf die entferntesten Dächer

Last Supper. Venetian. Sixteenth Century

I

As soon as I had finished my *Last Supper*
thirteen yards by five and a half,
a monstrous job, but rather well paid,
the usual questions came up:
What exactly are these foreigners doing here
with their halberds? They are dressed
like Germans, or like heretics.
Do you think it is normal
to depict Saint Luke
with a toothpick in his hand?
Who put the idea into your head
to sit Moors, drunkards and clowns
at Our Lord's table?
Do we have to put up with a dog
sniffing around, a dwarf, a parrot
and a Mameluke bleeding from his nose?
My Lords, I said, all this
I have invented for my own pleasure.
But the seven judges of the Holy Inquisition,
in a flutter of red silk robes,
murmured: That's as may be.

II

Oh, I have done better than that
in other paintings,
but nobody else can do a sky
the colour of this one;
and I am pleased by these cooks
with their long butcher's knives,
by these men clad in slashed hoods
trimmed with fur, in aigrets
adorned with heron feathers, in diadems
and pearl-studded turbans;
not to mention the muffled people

meiner Alabaster-Pälaste geklettert sind
und sich über die höchsten Brüstungen beugen.
Wonach sie Ausschau halten,
das weiß ich nicht. Aber weder euch
noch den Heiligen schenken sie einen Blick.

III

Wie oft soll ich es euch noch sagen!
Es gibt keine Kunst ohne das Vergnügen.
Das gilt auch für die endlosen Kreuzigungen,
Sintfluten und Bethlehemitischen Kindermorde,
die ihr, ich weiß nicht warum,
bei mir bestellt.
Als die Seufzer der Kritiker,
die Spitzfindigkeiten der Inquisitoren
und die Schnüffeleien der Schriftgelehrten
mir endlich zu dumm wurden,
taufte ich das *Letzte Abendmahl* um
und nannte es
Ein Dîner bei Herrn Levi.

IV

Wir werden ja sehen, wer den längeren Atem hat.
Zum Beispiel meine *Heilige Anna selbdritt.*
Kein sehr amüsantes Sujet.
Doch unter den Thron,
auf den herrlich gemusterten Marmorboden
in Sandrosa, Schwarz und Malachit,
malte ich, um das Ganze zu retten,
eine Suppenschildkröte mit rollenden Augen,
zierlichen Füßen und einem Panzer
aus halb durchsichtigem Schildpatt:
eine wunderbare Idee.
Wie ein riesiger, kunstvoll gewölbter Kamm,
topasfarben, glühte sie in der Sonne.

who have mounted the most distant rooftops
of my alabaster-faced palaces,
leaning over the parapets at a dizzy height.
What they are looking for
I cannot tell. But they do not even glance
at you, or at the saints.

III

I have told you again and again:
There is no art without pleasure.
This is true even of the endless Crucifixions,
Deluges and Massacres of the Innocent
which you ask me to execute –
I cannot imagine why.
So when the sighs of the critics,
the subtleties of the inquisitors
and the probings of the scribes
became too much for me,
I rechristened my *Last Supper*
and decided to call it
A Dinner at Mr Levi's.

IV

Just wait and see who will have the last word.
Take my *Saint Anne, the Virgin and Child*, for example.
Not a very amusing subject.
But underneath the throne,
on the checkered marble floor
done in sand-rose, black and malachite,
I put, as a redeeming grace,
a soup turtle with rolling eyes,
elegant feet and a shield
of translucent tortoiseshell.
A marvellous idea.
Like an enormous, perfectly arched shell comb,
the colour of topaz, she glowed in the sun.

V

Als ich sie kriechen sah,
fielen mir meine Feinde ein.
Ich hörte das Gebrabbel der Galeristen,
das Zischeln der Zeichenlehrer
und das Rülpsen der Besserwisser.

Ich nahm meinen Pinsel zur Hand
und begrub das Geschöpf,
bevor die Schmarotzer anfangen konnten,
mir zu erklären, was es bedeute,
unter sorgfältig gemalten Fliesen
aus schwarzem, grünem und rosa Marmor.
Die *Heilige Anna* ist nicht mein berühmtestes,
aber vielleicht mein bestes Bild.
Keiner außer mir weiß, warum.

V

But as soon as I saw her crawling,
I thought of my enemies.
The gallerists babbling,
the academicians hissing,
and the belching of the prigs.

I took up my brush
and I buried my creature
beneath a few carefully done tiles
of black, green and rose-coloured marble
before the parasites had a chance
to explain her to me.
Saint Anne is not my most famous work,
but perhaps my best.
No one except me knows why.

Innere Sicherheit

Ich versuche den Deckel zu heben,
logischerweise, den Deckel,
der meine Kiste verschließt.
Es ist ja kein Sarg, das nicht,
es ist nur eine Packung, eine Kabine,
mit einem Wort, eine Kiste.

Ihr wißt doch genau, was ich meine,
wenn ich *Kiste* sage,
stellt euch nicht dumm,
ich meine ja nur
eine ganz gewöhnliche Kiste,
auch nicht dunkler als eure.

Also ich möchte raus, ich klopfe,
ich hämmere gegen den Deckel,
ich rufe *Mehr Licht*, ich ringe
nach Atem, logischerweise,
ich donnere gegen die Luke. Gut.

Aber sicherheitshalber ist sie zu,
meine Kiste, sie geht nicht auf,
mein Schuhkarton hat einen Deckel,
der Deckel aber ist ziemlich schwer,
aus Sicherheitsgründen,
denn es handelt sich hier
um einen Behälter, um eine Bundeslade,
um einen Safe. Ich schaffe es nicht.

Die Befreiung kann, logischerweise,
nur mit vereinter Kraft gelingen.
Aber sicherheitshalber bin ich
in meiner Kiste mit mir allein,
in meiner eigenen Kiste.

Security Considerations

I am trying to lift the lid,
logically, the lid
on my private crate.
It isn't a coffin by any means,
it is just a package, a cabin, or
in a word, a crate.

You know what I mean
when I say *crate*, come on,
don't play the fool,
all I mean
is an average crate,
just as dark as your own.

Of course I want to get out,
and therefore I knock,
I hammer against the lid,
I call out *More light*, I gasp,
logically, pounding away at the hatch.

So far so good. Unfortunately,
for security reasons,
my crate does not open,
my shoe box has a lid,
a rather heavy one to be sure,
for security reasons,
since we are dealing here
with a container, an Ark
of the Covenant, a safe.
There is no way out.

For our liberation, joint action
would, logically, be needed.
But for security reasons
I am all alone in my crate,
in my very own crate.

Jedem das Seine! Um mit vereinter Kraft
zu entweichen aus der eigenen Kiste,
müßte ich, logischerweise, bereits
aus der eigenen Kiste
entwichen sein, und das gilt,
logischerweise, für alle.

Also stemme ich mich gegen den Deckel
mit meinem eignen Genick. Jetzt!
Einen Spalt breit! Ah! Draußen,
herrlich, die weite Landschaft,
bedeckt mit Büchsen, Kanistern,
kurzum, mit Kisten, dahinter
die eifrig rollenden grünen Fluten,
durchpflügt von seetüchtigen Koffern,
die unerhört hohen Wolken darüber,
und überall, überall Luft!

Laßt mich raus, rufe ich also,
erlahmend, wider besseres Wissen,
mit belegter Zunge, von Schweiß bedeckt.
Ein Kreuz schlagen, kommt nicht in Frage.
Winken, geht nicht, keine Hand frei.
Die Faust ballen, ausgeschlossen.

Also, *Ich drücke*, rufe ich,
mein Bedauern aus, wehe mir!
mein eignes Bedauern,
während mit dumpfem *Pflupp*
der Deckel sich wieder,
aus Sicherheitsgründen,
über mir schließt.

To every man his due! And hence,
for me to escape, by joint action,
from my own crate, logically
I would have to be out of it
to start with, and this condition obtains,
logically, for all of us.

Thus I break my very own back
against the lid. Now!
A chink, a narrow gap! Ah!
Marvellous! The open country
outside, covered with tins,
containers, or just plain crates,
in the background the high-rolling waves
ploughed by seaworthy trunks,
the enormously distant clouds above,
and lots and lots of fresh air!

Let me out, I proceed to cry,
feebly, with my tongue coated, against
my better judgement, covered with sweat.
To make the sign of the cross: impossible.
To beckon: no, I am short of hands.
To clench the fist: out of the question.

And hence I cry: *I express*
my regrets, woe to me,
my very own regrets,
while with a hollow *plop*
the lid, for security reasons,
comes down again
over my head.

Der Aufschub

Bei dem berühmten Ausbruch des Helgafell, eines Vulkans
auf der Insel Heimaey, live übertragen von einem Dutzend
hustender Fernsehteams, sah ich, unter dem Schwefelregen,
einen älteren Mann in Hosenträgern, der, achselzuckend
und ohne sich weiter zu kümmern um Sturmwind, Hitze,
Kameraleute, Asche, Zuschauer (unter ihnen auch ich
vor dem bläulichen Bildschirm auf meinem Teppich).
mit einem Gartenschlauch, dünn aber deutlich sichtbar,
gegen die Lava vorging, bis endlich Nachbarn, Soldaten,
Schulkinder, ja sogar Feuerwehrleute mit Schläuchen,
immer mehr Schläuchen, gegen die heiße, unaufhaltsam
vorrückende Lava eine Mauer aus naß erstarrter
kalter Lava höher und höher türmten, und so,
zwar aschgrau und nicht für immer, doch einstweilen,
den Untergang des Abendlandes aufschoben, dergestalt,
daß, falls sie nicht gestorben sind, auf Heimaey,
einer Insel unweit von Island, heute noch diese Leute
in ihren kleinen bunten Holzhäusern morgens erwachen
und nachmittags, unbeachtet von Kameras, den Salat
in ihren Gärten, lavagedüngt und riesenköpfig,
sprengen, vorläufig nur, natürlich, doch ohne Panik.

The Reprieve

Watching the famous eruption of a volcano on Heimaey, Iceland,
which was broadcast live by any number of TV teams,
I saw an elderly man in braces showered by sulphur and brimstone,
ignoring the storm, the heat, the video cables, the ash
and the spectators (including myself, crouching on my carpet
in front of the livid screen), who held a garden hose,
slender but clearly visible, aimed at the roaring lava,
until neighbours joined him, soldiers, children, firemen,
pointing more and more hoses at the advancing fiery lava
and turning it into a towering wall, higher and higher,
of lava, hard, cold and wet, the colour of ash, and thus postponing,
not forever perhaps, but for the time being at least,
the Decline of Western Civilisation, which is why
the people of Heimaey, unless they have died since,
continue to dwell unmolested by cameras
in their dapper white wooden houses,
calmly watering in the afternoon
the lettuce in their gardens, which, thanks to the blackened soil,
has grown simply enormous, and for the time being at least,
fails to show any signs of impending disaster.

Schwacher Trost

Der Kampf aller gegen alle soll,
wie aus Kreisen verlautet,
die dem Innenministerium nahestehn,
demnächst verstaatlicht werden,
bis auf den letzten Blutfleck.
Schöne Grüße von Hobbes.

Bürgerkrieg mit ungleichen Waffen:
was dem einen die Steuererklärung,
ist dem andern die Fahrradkette.
Die Giftmischer und die Brandstifter
werden eine Gewerkschaft gründen müssen
zum Schutz ihrer Arbeitsplätze.

Aufgeschlossen bis dort hinaus
geht es im Strafvollzug zu.
Abwaschbar, in schwarzes Plastik gebunden,
liegt Kropotkin zum Studium aus:
*System der gegenseitigen Hilfe
in der Natur.* Ein schwacher Trost.

Wir haben mit Bedauern vernommen,
daß es keine Gerechtigkeit gibt,
und mit noch größerem Bedauern,
daß es, wie die bewußten Kreise
händereibend versichern, auch nichts
dergleichen je geben kann, soll und wird.

Strittig ist nach wie vor, wer oder was
daran schuld sei. Ist es die Erbsünde
oder die Genetik? die Säuglingspflege?
der Mangel an Herzensbildung?
die falsche Diät? der Gottseibeiuns?
die Männerherrschaft? das Kapital?

Cold Comfort

Man's struggle against man,
according to reliable sources
close to the Home Office,
will be nationalised in due course,
down to the last bloodstain.
Kind regards from Thomas Hobbes.

A civil war fought with unequal arms:
one man's tax return
is another man's bicycle chain.
Poisoners and incendiaries
are planning to form a union
and call for job protection.

Our prison service
is utterly open-minded.
They offer Kropotkin's *System
of Mutual Aid in the Natural World*,
bound in washable black plastic covers,
as a study course. This is cold comfort.

We have learned to our dismay
that there is no justice,
and furthermore, to our even greater dismay,
from informed sources beaming with satisfaction,
that nothing remotely like it
can, should or will ever exist.

It is not yet quite clear
whose fault this may be. Original Sin?
Genetics? Methods of infant care?
The lack of polite education?
Capitalism? Unhealthy diet?
The Devil? Or Male Domination?

Daß wir es leider nicht lassen können,
einander zu notzüchtigen,
an die nächstbeste Kreuzung zu nageln
und die Überreste zu essen, schön wär es,
dafür eine Erklärung zu finden,
Balsam für die Vernunft.

Zwar die tägliche Scheußlichkeit stört,
doch sie wundert uns wenig.
Was aber rätselhaft anmutet, ist
die stille Handreichung,
die grundlose Gutmütigkeit,
sowie die englische Sanftmut.

Also höchste Zeit, mit feuriger Zunge
den Kellner zu loben, der stundenlang
der Tirade des Impotenten lauscht;
den Barmherzigkeit übenden Knäckebrot-
Vertreter, der kurz vor dem tödlichen Schlag
den Zahlungsbefehl sinken läßt;

wie auch die Betschwester, die,
unverhofft, den atemlos an ihre Tür
hämmernden Deserteur versteckt;
und den Entführer, der sein wirres Werk
mit einem matten, zufriedenen Lächeln
unversehens aufgibt, zu Tode erschöpft;

und wir legen die Zeitung weg
und freuen uns, achselzuckend, so,
wie wenn der Schmachtfetzen glücklich aus ist,
wenn es hell wird im Kino, und draußen
hat es zu regnen aufgehört, dann blüht uns
endlich der erste Zug aus der Zigarette.

Unfortunately we cannot refrain
from rape and from ravishment,
from nailing each other down
to the nearest crosswalk
and from gobbling up the remains.
To find out why would be nice,
balm on the wounds of Reason.

We are annoyed but not surprised
by our daily atrocities.
What we find puzzling
are mild ministrations,
groundless generosity
and angelical sweetness.

It is therefore high time
to praise with fiery tongues
the waiter listening for hours on end
to the impotent man's lamentation:
the biscuit salesman showing mercy
and tearing up at the last moment
the writ of execution;

the bigoted spinster hiding,
strangely enough, the deserter
hammering breathlessly at her door;
and the kidnapper, suddenly tired
to death, giving up his tangled work
with a feeble, contented smile.

With a shrug we put the newspaper down,
filled with joy, the kind of joy
we feel when the B-picture
finally draws to an end, the lights
come on in the cinema, outside
the rain has stopped, and we long
for our first puff of smoke.

Weitere Gründe dafür, daß die Dichter lügen

Weil der Augenblick,
in dem das Wort *glücklich*
ausgesprochen wird,
niemals der glückliche Augenblick ist.
Weil der Verdurstende seinen Durst
nicht über die Lippen bringt.
Weil im Munde der Arbeiterklasse
das Wort *Arbeiterklasse* nicht vorkommt.
Weil, wer verzweifelt,
nicht Lust hat, zu sagen:
»Ich bin ein Verzweifelnder.«
Weil Orgasmus und *Orgasmus*
nicht miteinander vereinbar sind.
Weil der Sterbende, statt zu behaupten:
»Ich sterbe jetzt«,
nur ein mattes Geräusch vernehmen läßt,
das wir nicht verstehen.
Weil es die Lebenden sind,
die den Toten in den Ohren liegen
mit ihren Schreckensnachrichten.
Weil die Wörter zu spät kommen,
oder zu früh.
Weil es also ein anderer ist,
immer ein anderer,
der da redet,
und weil der,
von dem da die Rede ist,
schweigt.

Further Reasons Why Poets Do Not Tell the Truth

Because the moment
when the word *happy*
is pronounced
never is the moment of happiness.
Because the thirsty man
does not give mouth to his thirst.
Because *proletariat* is a word
which will not pass the lips of the proletariat.
Because he who despairs
does not feel like saying:
'I am desperate.'
Because orgasm and *orgasm*
are worlds apart.
Because the dying man,
far from proclaiming:
'I die,' only utters
a faint rattle,
which we fail to comprehend.
Because it is the living
who batter the ears of the dead
with their atrocities.
Because words come always
too late or too soon.
Because it is someone else,
always someone else,
who does the talking,
and because he
who is being talked about,
keeps his silence.

Nur die Ruhe

Zuweilen, wenn auch nicht oft, sieht man im Schnee,
bei winterlichen Hasenjagden, oder, kurz vor Ostern,
durch das halb geöffnete Schlafwagenfenster,
während es hell wird draußen, auf Scheunendächern,
Kohlenhalden, Bismarcktürmen im Mischwald,
kleine Schwärme von schwarz gekleideten Leuten,
angeführt von einem Propheten, die Nickelbrille
auf den geblähten Nüstern, unbeweglich verharren
in Erwartung des Weltunterganges. Während wir andern,
beschäftigt mit unsern wichtigen Kinkerlitzchen,
die Sintflut im fernsten Perfekt vermuten,
oder wir halten sie gar für eine ehrwürdige Ente,
wissen jene, im Hochsitz lauernd, auf die Minute genau,
Wann. Rechtzeitig haben sie ihre Fernseher abgemeldet,
den Kühlschrank ausgeräumt, damit nichts verdirbt,
und ihre Seele gerüstet. Erschütternd dünn
wehn uns ihre Stimmchen ins Ohr über die bereinigte Flur,
den Ruhrschnellweg, den kühlen, baureifen Wiesengrund:
Näher, mein Gott, zu Dir. Auf die Dauer freilich
wird es kaum zu vermeiden sein, daß der eine
oder der andere auf die Uhr blickt und stutzt;
daß dem Propheten der mahnend erhobene Arm lahmt;
und daß, während es aufklart, der D-Zug vorbeirappelt,
die Halden schrumpfen, der Schnee schmilzt
und die Hasen in die Bratröhre wandern, einer
nach dem andern sich, unter dem höhnischen Beifall
der Mitwelt, wieder abseilen wird in den niederen Alltag,
das Gehaltkonto neu eröffnen, eine Gießkanne kaufen,
sich gefaßt machen auf den unvermeidlichen Urlaub.
Angesichts der Allgemeinen Geschäftsbedingungen
und der schmutzigen Wäsche muß sogar der Prophet
gewisse Zugeständnisse machen, aber hart bleibt er
in der Sache. Mit dünner doch fester Stimme sagt er sich:
Das sind alles Äußerlichkeiten. Nur Geduld!
Ein paar Wochen oder Jahrhunderte hin oder her,
was verschlägt das schon im Vergleich mit der Ewigkeit.

Keeping Cool

Sometimes, not very frequently, hunting hares in the winter,
you will perceive in the snow, or shortly before Easter,
peering through the half-open window of your sleeping car,
against the dawning day, on the roof of a lonely barn,
on a pile of coal, or on a belvedere across the valley,
a small flock of people dressed in black coats,
led by a prophet with steel-rimmed spectacles
and flared nostrils, motionless, silent, waiting
for Doom to come. We, of course, go on bothering
about our humdrum business, supposing the deluge
to be something antediluvian, or else
an elaborate practical joke – while they, perched
on their respective lookouts, know exactly the moment
When. They have returned their hired cars in good time,
emptied their fridges and prepared their souls.
Terribly thin is the sound of their voices,
swept by the wind across the freeway, the shady dell
due for development: 'Nearer, my God, to Thee.'
In the long run, however, it can hardly be helped
that first one, then another will glance at his watch
and be taken aback; the prophet's arm, raised in admonition,
will go to sleep; and while the weak sun rises,
the train passes by, the coal is burnt up,
the snow melts away and the hares end up in the oven,
first one, then another will slowly come down
and join us in the nether regions of routine,
meeting the mockery of the commonplace,
buying a toothbrush, reopening his bank account
and bracing himself for the inevitable holidays.
Even the prophet himself, faced with the small print
and with dirty linen, will have to make allowances,
hanging on, however, to the essentials.
His voice may crack but it does not fail him.
Outward appearances do not matter. What are weeks
or even centuries, compared to Eternity?

Was ihn betrifft, er wird, wenn es einst soweit ist,
keineswegs überrascht sein. Von jeher schließlich
hat er sich auf den Standpunkt gestellt: So
kann es nicht weitergehen! Recht werde uns geschehen!
Selber schuld! Hätten wir nur beizeiten auf ihn gehört!
Und also fühlt er auf seinem Scheunendach, unverzagt
krähend, daß der Weltuntergang immer aufs neue,
und wäre er noch so unpünktlich, mundet wie Manna,
daß er eine Art von Beruhigung ist, ein süßer Trost
bei trüber Aussicht, bei Haarausfall, und bei nassen Füßen.

He for his part will not be surprised
by the Day of Reckoning. I told you so, he will mutter.
Things just couldn't go on like this. But unfortunately
nobody listened to me. And thus even now he feels,
perched on the top of his barn and crowing away,
that Doom, however unpunctual, will always be
a tranquilliser of sorts, a sweet consolation
for dull prospects, loss of hair, and wet feet.

Erkenntnistheoretisches Modell

Hier hast du
eine große Schachtel
mit der Aufschrift
Schachtel.
Wenn du sie öffnest,
findest du darin
eine Schachtel
mit der Aufschrift
Schachtel
aus einer Schachtel
mit der Aufschrift
Schachtel.
Wenn du sie öffnest –
ich meine jetzt
diese Schachtel,
nicht jene –,
findest du darin
eine Schachtel
mit der Aufschrift
Und so weiter,
und wenn du
so weiter machst,
findest du
nach unendlichen Mühen
eine unendlich kleine
Schachtel
mit einer Aufschrift
so winzig,
daß sie dir gleichsam
vor den Augen
verdunstet.
Es ist eine Schachtel,
die nur in deiner Einbildung
existiert.
Eine vollkommen leere
Schachtel.

Model toward a Theory of Cognition

Here is a box for you,
a large box
labelled
Box.
Open it,
and you will find
a box in it,
labelled
Box from a box
labelled Box.
Look into it
(I mean this box now,
not the other one),
and you will find a box
labelled
And so on,
and if you go on
like this,
you will find,
after infinite efforts,
an infinitely small
box
with a label
so tiny
that the lettering,
as it were,
dissolves
before your eyes.
It is a box
existing only
in your imagination.
A perfectly empty
box.

Erkennungsdienstliche Behandlung

Das ist nicht Dante.

Das ist eine Photographie von Dante.

Das ist ein Film, in dem ein Schauspieler auftritt, der vorgibt, Dante zu sein.

Das ist ein Film, in dem Dante Dante spielt.

Das ist ein Mann, der von Dante träumt.

Das ist ein Mann, der Dante heißt, aber nicht Dante ist.

Das ist ein Mann, der Dante nachäfft.

Das ist ein Mann, der sich für Dante ausgibt.

Das ist ein Mann, der träumt, er sei Dante.

Das ist ein Mann, der Dante zum Verwechseln ähnlich sieht.

Das ist eine Wachsfigur von Dante.

Das ist ein Wechselbalg, ein Zwilling, ein Doppelgänger.

Das ist ein Mann, der sich für Dante hält.

Das ist ein Mann, den alle, außer Dante, für Dante halten.

Das ist ein Mann, den alle für Dante halten, nur er selber glaubt nicht daran.

Das ist ein Mann, den niemand für Dante hält außer Dante.

Das ist Dante.

Identity Check

This is not Dante.
This is a photograph of Dante.
This is a film showing an actor who pretends to be Dante.
This is a film with Dante in the role of Dante.
This is a man who dreams of Dante.
This is a man called Dante who is not Dante.
This is a man who apes Dante.
This is a man who passes himself off as Dante.
This is a man who dreams that he is Dante.
This is a man who is the very spit image of Dante.
This is a wax figure of Dante.
This is a changeling, a double, an identical twin.
This is a man who believes he is Dante.
This is a man everybody, except Dante, believes to be Dante.
This is a man everybody believes to be Dante, only he himself
    does not fall for it.
This is a man nobody believes to be Dante, except Dante.
This is Dante.

Forschungsgemeinschaft

O Propheten mit dem Rücken zum Meer,
mit dem Rücken zur Gegenwart, o seelenruhig
in die Zukunft blickende Zauberkünstler,
o immerfort an die Reling gelehnte Schamanen –
einmal ein Taschenbuch durchgeblättert,
das genügt, um euch zu begreifen!

Aus Knochen lesen, aus Sternen, aus Scherben,
zum Wohle der Allgemeinheit, aus Eingeweiden,
was gewesen ist und was bevorsteht –
O Wissenschaft! Gebenedeit seist du,
gebenedeit deine kleinen Lichtblicke,
halb Bluff halb Statistik: Todesarten,
Geldmengenziele, wachsende Entropie...

Weiter so! Diese schwefelgelben Erleuchtungen
sind besser als nichts, sie unterhalten uns
an dunstigen Sommerabenden:
Papierbahnen frisch vom Computer,
Stichproben, Ausgrabungen, Tips
nach der Delphi-Methode – bravo!

Gebenedeit sei das Vorläufige!
Vorläufig ist noch genug frisches Wasser da,
vorläufig atmet und lauscht die Haut,
deine Haut, meine, – sogar die eure,
ihr holzigen Medizinmänner, atmet noch,
ungeachtet der Bleibeverhandlungen,
der Fußnoten und des Stellenkegels –
vorläufig ist das Ende (»eine unaufhörliche,
feinverteilte Naturkatastrophe«)
noch nicht endgültig – das ist angenehm!

Also am Wochenende, liebe Mitwisser,
– vor Neufundland vereinzelt Eisberge,
über Mitteleuropa Sommergewitter,

Research Council

O prophets with your backs turned to the sea,
with your backs turned to the present, O sorcerers
looking placidly into the future,
O shaman priests forever leaning over the railing –
one single paperback leafed through
is enough to see through your mysteries!

Reading in bones, in stars, in debris,
from entrails, all that has been and all
that is bound to happen, for the public good,
O Science! be blessed and blessed be
the rather minor rays of light which you offer us,
half bluff and half statistics: mortalities,
money supply targets, increasing entropy...

Carry on! All these brimstone-coloured illuminations
are better than nothing at all,
they keep us happy on sultry summer nights:
computer print-outs fresh from the backroom,
sample probes, excavations, tip-offs
based on the Delphi method – hear, hear!

Blessed be your interim reports!
For the time being there is enough fresh water left,
the skin is still breathing expectantly,
my skin twitches, our skin, and even yours,
you dead-alive medicine men,
notwithstanding the question of tenure,
the footnotes and the likelihood of advancement –
for the time being the end (an interminable,
finely scattered act of God)
is not yet final – a comforting thought!

And hence, my dear accessories before the fact,
while off Newfoundland icebergs are being forecast
and thunderstorms in the sulphur-lined skies

schweflig am dunstigen Horizont –
nichts wie raus aus den Instituten!
Ein bißchen Leben am Wochenende,
was immer das heißen mag, vorläufig
natürlich nur, und ohne prognostischen Wert.

O ihr ewig nach Erkenntnissen Dürstenden,
ihr dauert mich, wie ihr dann auf der Datscha.
im irischen Bauernhaus, auf Korčula,
mit dem Rücken zum Meer, seelenruhig
euer Gehirn ausklinkt – daß euch allerdings
beim Ping-Pong die Fackel nicht ausgehe!
Nur so weiter! Ich segne euch.

of Central Europe, you had better get out
of your institutes for the weekend. Run
for your life, or a slice of it, an interim,
whatever that may mean, until Monday;
though as a basis for your predictions
this course of action may not be much good.

O my friends, ever thirsting for knowledge,
I pity you, resting at your dachas,
your Irish cottages, or in Korčula,
turning your backs on the sea
and switching your brains off, placidly.
Onward, and may your torch never go out
during the ping-pong match! I bless you.

Fachschaft Philosophie

Daß wir gescheit sind, ist wahr. Aber weit entfernt,
die Welt zu verändern, ziehen wir auf dem Podium
Kaninchen aus unserm Gehirn, Kaninchen und Tauben,
Schwärme von schneeweißen Tauben, die unverwandt
auf die Bücher kacken. Daß Vernunft Vernunft ist
und nicht Vernunft, um das zu kapieren,
braucht man nicht Hegel zu sein, dazu genügt
ein Blick in den Taschenspiegel. Er zeigt uns
in wallenden blauen Mäntelchen, bestickt
mit silbernen Sternen, und auf dem Kopf
einen spitzen Hut. Im Keller versammeln wir uns,
wo die Karteileichen liegen, zum Hegelkongreß,
packen unsre Kristallkugeln und Horoskope aus
und machen uns an die Arbeit. Gutachten
schwenken wir, Pendel, Forschungsberichte,
wir lassen die Tische rücken, wir fragen:
Wie wirklich ist das, was wirklich ist? Schadenfroh
lächelt Hegel. Wir malen ihm einen Schnurrbart an.
Schon sieht er wie Stalin aus. Der Kongreß
tanzt. Weit und breit kein Vulkan. Unauffällig
stehen die Posten Posten. In aller Ruhe wirft,
Knüppel aus dem Sack, unser psychischer Apparat
treffende Sätze aus, und wir sagen uns:
In jedem brutalen Bullen steckt doch
ein verständnisvoller Helfer und Freund,
in dem ein brutaler Bulle steckt. Simsalabim!
Wie ein enormes Taschentuch entfalten wir
die Theorie, während vor dem verbunkerten Seminar
bescheiden die Herren im Trenchcoat warten.
Sie rauchen, machen kaum Gebrauch von der Dienstwaffe,
und bewachen die Planstellen, die Papierblumen
und den schneeweiß alles bedeckenden Taubendreck.

Dept. of Philosophy

No doubt we are intelligent. But far
from changing the face of the world, on stage
we keep producing rabbits from our brains
and snow-white pigeons, swarms of pigeons
who invariably shit on the books.
You don't have to be Hegel to catch on to the fact
that Reason is both reasonable and against Reason.
All it takes is a look into your pocket mirror.
You will see yourself wearing a blue gown,
spangled with silver stars, and a pointed hat.
For the Hegel Congress we meet in the cellar
where our card-file colleagues are buried,
unpack our crystal balls and our horoscopes,
and go to work, waving our expertise,
our pendulum and our research reports.
We make the tables turn, we ask reality
How real is it? Hegel is smiling,
filled with *schadenfreude*. We daub his face
with an inky moustache. He now looks like Stalin.
The congress is having a ball, but there is
no volcano in sight to dance on. The guards
outside are on their guard. Our pysche
calmly produces pertinent statements,
and we agree that deep down in any given brutal pig
a well-meaning public servant is to be found
and the other way round. Abracadabra!
Like an enormous handkerchief we unfold
our theories. The plainclothes men
in their trench coats are modestly waiting
in front of the riot-proof seminar shelter.
They smoke, they hardly ever make use of their guns,
they keep guard on our faculty roster, our paper flowers
and the snow-white pigeon droppings all over the place.

Die Ruhe auf der Flucht. Flämisch, 1521

Ich sehe das spielende Kind im Korn,
das den Bären nicht sieht.
Der Bär umarmt oder schlägt einen Bauern.
Den Bauern sieht er,
aber er sieht das Messer nicht,
das in seinem Rücken steckt;
nämlich im Rücken des Bären.

Auf dem Hügel drüben liegen die Überreste
eines Geräderten; doch der Spielmann,
der vorübergeht, weiß nichts davon.
Auch bemerken die beiden Heere,
die auf der hell erleuchteten Ebene
gegeneinander vorrücken –
ihre Lanzen funkeln und blenden mich –,
den kreisenden Sperber nicht,
der sie ins kalte Auge faßt.

Ich sehe deutlich die Schimmelfäden,
die sich durch das Dachgebälk ziehen,
im Vordergrund, und weiter hinten
den vorbeisprengenden Kurier.
Aus einem Hohlweg muß er aufgetaucht sein.
Niemals werde ich wissen,
wie dieser Hohlweg von innen aussieht;
aber ich denke mir,
daß er feucht ist, schattig und feucht.

Die Schwäne auf dem Teich in der Mitte des Bildes
nehmen keine Notiz von mir.
Ich betrachte den Tempel am Abgrund,
den schwarzen Elefanten – seltsam,
ein schwarzer Elefant auf freiem Feld! –
und die Statuen, deren weiße Augen
dem Vogelfänger im Wald zusehen,

The Rest on the Flight. Flemish, 1521

I see the child playing in the corn,
who does not see the bear.
I see the bear hugging or killing a peasant.
He sees the peasant,
but not the knife
sticking in his back,
that is, in the back of the bear.

On the hill over there lie the remains
of a man who was put to the wheel;
but the minstrel passing by
does not notice them.
As for the two legions
advancing upon each other
on the brightly lit plain,
the flash of their lances is blinding me,
but they fail to observe the hawk circling overhead
who keeps a cold eye on them.

I distinguish the threads of mould
dangling from the roof beam
in the foreground, and in the distance
I perceive the courier galloping by.
He must have emerged from a ravine.
Never shall I come to know
what this ravine looks like from within;
but I imagine that it is damp,
very damp, and full of shadows.

To the centre of the picture the swans
in the pond ignore me.
I see the temple on the edge of the precipice,
the black elephant on guard
(how strange to see a black elephant in the open fields!)
and the statues, who out of their white eyes
watch the fowler in the forest,

dem Fährmann, der Feuersbrunst.
Wie lautlos das alles ist!

Auf sehr entlegenen, sehr hohen Türmen
mit fremdartigen Schießscharten
seh ich die Eulen zwinkern. Ja,
dies alles sehe ich wohl,
doch worauf es ankommt, das weiß ich nicht.
Wie sollte ich es erraten,
da alles das, was ich sehe,
so deutlich ist, so notwendig
und so undurchdringlich?

Nichts ahnend, in meine Geschäfte versunken
wie in die ihrigen jene Stadt,
oder wie weit in der Ferne
jene noch viel blaueren Städte
verschwimmend in andern Erscheinungen,
andern Wolken, Heeren und Ungeheuern,
lebe ich weiter. Ich gehe fort.
Ich habe dies alles gesehen, nur
das Messer, das mir im Rücken steckt, nicht.

the ferryman, and the conflagration.
How silently all these things come to pass!

On very remote, lofty towers
with uncommon embrasures
I see the owls winking. O yes,
all these things I can well see,
but how should I know what matters
and what does not? How should I guess?
Everything here seems evident,
equally distinct, necessary
and impenetrable.

Out of my depth, lost in my own concerns,
just like the faraway city over there,
and like those other cities, even bluer
and even more distant,
dissolving into other visions,
other clouds, legions and monsters,
I go on living. I go away.
I have seen all this, but I cannot see
the knife sticking in my back.

THE FURY OF DISAPPEARANCE

DIE FURIE DES VERSCHWINDENS

(1980)

Die Dreiunddreißigjährige

Sie hat sich das alles ganz anders vorgestellt.
Immer diese verrosteten Volkswagen.
Einmal hätte sie fast einen Bäcker geheiratet.
Erst hat sie Hesse gelesen, dann Handke.
Jetzt löst sie öfter Silbenrätsel im Bett.
Von Männern läßt sie sich nichts gefallen.
Jahrelang war sie Trotzkistin, aber auf ihre Art.
Sie hat nie eine Brotmarke in der Hand gehabt.
Wenn sie an Kambodscha denkt, wird ihr ganz schlecht.
Ihr letzter Freund, der Professor, wollte immer verhaut werden.
Grünliche Batik-Kleider, die ihr zu weit sind.
Blattläuse auf der Zimmerlinde.
Eigentlich wollte sie malen, oder auswandern.
Ihre Dissertation, *Klassenkämpfe in Ulm, 1500*
bis 1512, und ihre Spuren im Volkslied:
Stipendien, Anfänge und ein Koffer voller Notizen.
Manchmal schickt ihr die Großmutter Geld.
Zaghafte Tänze im Badezimmer, kleine Grimassen,
stundenlang Gurkenmilch vor dem Spiegel.
Sie sagt: Ich werde schon nicht verhungern.
Wenn sie weint, sieht sie aus wie neunzehn.

At Thirty-Three

It was all so different from what she'd expected.
Always those rusting Volkswagens.
At one time she'd almost married a baker.
First she read Hesse, then Handke.
Now often she does crosswords in bed.
With her, men take no liberties.
For years she was a Trotskyist, but in her own way.
She's never handled a ration card.
When she thinks of Kampuchea she feels quite sick.
Her last lover, the professor, always wanted her to beat him.
Greenish batik dresses, always too wide for her.
Greenflies on her *Sparmannia*.
Really she wanted to paint, or emigrate.
Her thesis, *Class Struggles in Ulm 1500*
to 1512 and References to them in Folksong:
Grants, beginnings and a suitcase full of notes.
Sometimes her grandmother sends her money.
Tentative dances in her bathroom, little grimaces,
cucumber juice for hours in front of the mirror.
She says, whatever happpens I shan't starve.
When she weeps she looks like nineteen.

Der Angestellte

Nie hat et jemanden umgebracht. Nein,
er wirft aus Versehen Flaschen um.
Er möchte gern, schwitzt, verliert
seinen liebsten Schlüssel. Immerzu
erkältet er sich. Er weiß, daß er muß.
Er mutet sich Mut zu, er gähnt,
er tupft seinen Gram auf den Putz.
Er denkt, lieber nicht. Eingezwängt
in zwei Schuhe, beteuert er bleich
das Gegenteil. Ja, er meldet sich an
und ab. Das Gegenteil sagt er von dem,
was er sagen wollte. Eigentlich, sagt er,
eigentlich nicht. Der Anzug ist ihm zu eng,
zu weit. Seine Stelle schmerzt. Nein,
seine eigene Handschrift kann er schon längst
nicht mehr lesen. Er hat sich scheiden lassen,
vergebens. Kein Mensch ruft ihn an. Überall
juckt es ihn. Sein Kugelschreiber läuft aus,
beim besten Willen. Er ist öfters vorhanden,
in jedem Zimmer einmal, immer allein.
Er schneidet sich beim Rasieren. Ja,
er paßt nämlich immer auf, sonst
kann er nicht schlafen. Er schläft.
Alles meckert, alles was recht ist,
alles lacht über ihn. Er merkt nicht,
was los ist. Das merkt er. Sein Kopfweh
ist unpolitisch. Er stellt sich an,
er stottert schon wieder, verschluckt sich.
Was er vorhin hat sagen wollen, das hat er
vorhin vergessen. Er hat vergessen,
sich umzubringen. Beim besten Willen.
Heimlich lebt er. Nein, er darf nicht,
aber er müßte. Er hat keinen Krebs,
aber das weiß er nicht. Sein Hut schwitzt.
Es ist ihm noch nie so gut gegangen
wie jetzt. Eigentlich möchte er nicht,

The Employee

He has never killed anyone. No,
he upsets bottles by accident.
He would like to, sweats, loses
his favourite key. All the time
he catches colds. He knows that he must.
He supposes he could be brave, he yawns,
he dabs his grief on to the stucco.
He thinks, better not. Jammed into
a pair of shoes, palely he asserts
the opposite. Yes, he reports himself in
and out. He says the opposite of
what he wanted to say. Really, he says,
really not. His suit is too tight for him,
too wide. His place hurts. No,
for a long time he has been unable
to read his own handwriting. He divorced,
in vain. No one rings him up. He itches
all over. His ball-pen runs out,
with the best will. He is often present,
once in each room, always alone.
He cuts himself shaving. Yes,
for he always takes care, otherwise
he can't sleep. He sleeps.
Everyone cackles, everyone who is right,
everyone laughs at him. He can't see
what's wrong. He sees it all right. His headache
is unpolitical. He tries hard,
he's stammering again, begins to choke.
What he wanted to say a moment ago, he
forgot a moment ago. He has forgotten
to do away with himself. With the best will.
Secretly he lives. No, he must not,
but he ought to. He doesn't have cancer
but he doesn't know that. His hat sweats.
He has never done as well
as he's doing now. Really, he'd rather not,

aber er muß. Er weint beim Friseur. Ja,
er ist anstellig, er entschuldigt sich.
Ja, er schreibt, ja, er kratzt sich,
ja, er müßte, aber er darf nicht,
nein, seinen Jammer hat niemand bemerkt.

but he must. He weeps at the hairdresser's. Yes,
he's efficient enough, he apologises.
Yes, he writes, yes, he scratches himself.
Yes, he ought to, but he mustn't.
No, his misery has not been noticed by anyone.

Die Scheidung

Erst war es nur ein unmerkliches Beben der Haut –
»Wie du meinst« –, dort wo das Fleisch am dunkelsten ist.
»Was hast du?« – Nichts. Milchige Träume
von Umarmungen, aber am anderen Morgen
sieht der andere anders aus, sonderbar knochig.
Messerscharfe Mißverständnisse. »Damals in Rom – «
Das habe ich nie gesagt. – Pause. Rasendes Herzklopfen,
eine Art Haß, sonderbar. – »Darum geht es nicht.«
Wiederholungen. Strahlend hell die Gewißheit:
Von nun an ist alles falsch. Geruchlos und scharf,
wie ein Paßfoto, diese unbekannte Person
mit dem Teeglas am Tisch, mit starren Augen.
Es hat keinen Zweck keinen Zweck keinen Zweck:
Litanei im Kopf, ein Anflug von Übelkeit.
Ende der Vorwürfe. Langsam füllt sich
das ganze Zimmer bis zur Decke mit Schuld.
Die klagende Stimme ist fremd, nur die Schuhe,
die krachend zu Boden fallen, die Schuhe nicht.
Das nächste Mal, in einem leeren Restaurant,
Zeitlupe, Brotbrösel, wird über Geld gesprochen,
lachend. Der Nachtisch schmeckt nach Metall.
Zwei Unberührbare. Schrille Vernunft.
»Alles halb so schlimm.« Aber nachts
die Rachsucht, der stumme Kampf, anonym,
wie zwei knochige Advokaten, zwei große Krebse
im Wasser. Dann die Erschöpfung. Langsam
blättert der Schorf ab. Ein neues Tabakgeschäft,
eine neue Adresse. Parias, schrecklich erleichtert.
Blasser werdende Schatten. Dies sind die Akten.
Dies ist der Schlüsselbund. Dies ist die Narbe.

The Divorce

At first it was only an imperceptible quivering of the skin –
'As you wish' – where the flesh is darkest.
'What's wrong with you?' – Nothing. Milky dreams
of embraces; next morning, though,
the other looks different, strangely bony.
Razor-sharp misunderstandings. 'That time, in Rome –'
I never said that. A pause. And furious palpitations,
a sort of hatred, strange. 'That's not the point.'
Repetitions. Radiantly clear, this certainty:
From now on all is wrong. Odourless and sharp,
like a passport photo, this unknown person
with a glass of tea at table, with staring eyes.
It's no good, no good, no good:
litany in the head, a slight nausea.
End of reproaches. Slowly the whole room
fills with guilt right up to the ceiling.
This complaining voice is strange, only not
the shoes that drop with a bang, not the shoes.
Next time, in an empty restaurant
slow motion, bread crumbs, money is discussed,
laughing. The dessert tastes of metal.
Two untouchables. Shrill reasonableness.
'Not so bad really.' But at night
the thoughts of vengeance, the silent fight, anonymous
like two bony barristers, two large crabs
in water. Then the exhaustion. Slowly
the scab peels off. A new tobacconist,
a new address. Pariahs, horribly relieved.
Shades growing paler. These are the documents.
This is the bunch of keys. This is the scar.

Der Urlaub

Jetzt, wo er frei hat, verhältnismäßig, schlurft er
oft um die Tennisplätze, läßt sich rasieren, liest.
Schwarzhändler wispern, Turnschuhe hecheln vorbei.
Starrend vor Palmen dehnt sich die Welt
am Sonntag. Im Palace brüten die ersten Huren
über dem Frühstück. Alles klar, alles fusselt.
Menschenskind, Mecki, ruft es vom Nebentisch.
Heulendes Elend am Strand. Umständehalber
schmelzen Peseten. Zufallsbekanntschaften,
sehnsüchtig eingekremt. »Was sagst du dazu, José,
wenn ich heut nacht mit dir geh? Olé, olé, olé.«
Ekelhaft, dieser Tintenfisch auf dem Teller.
Das gähnende Zimmer. Sand in den Handtüchern.
Ein helles Insekt, das sich gegen die Birne wirft.
Siebzehn senkrecht: Griechische Fruchtbarkeitsgöttin.
Die Dusche riecht muffig. Auf der Straße kichert es.
Motorräder starten. Dann ist nur noch das Meer da,
das in der Ferne ächzt. Nein, nebenan ist es,
nebenenan stirbt eine Frau oder liebt sich selbst.
Olé, olé, was sagst du dazu, José? Er horcht.
Weiß im Zahnputzglas wimmeln die Schlaftabletten.

The Holiday

Now that he's free, relatively, often he shuffles
round the tennis courts, pays for a shave, reads.
Black marketeers whisper, plimsolls pant past him.
Stiff with palm trees, the world expands
on Sundays. Here, in the Palace, the first whores
brood over their breakfast. All is clear, all fuzzes.
Well, if it isn't Nick! comes from the next table.
On the beach, howling misery. Complications
melt away pesetas. Chance acquaintances,
longingly primed with lotion. 'What do you say, José,
if tonight we go and play? Olé, olé, olé.'
Disgusting, this octopus on the plate.
The yawning bedroom. Sand in the towels.
A brilliant insect that collides with the lighbulb.
At seventeen degrees: Greek fertility goddess.
The shower smells musty. In the street someone titters.
Motorbikes rev. Then there's only the sea
that sighs away into the distance. No, it's the next room,
in the next room a woman is dying or loving herself.
Olé, olé what do you say, José? He listens.
White in his tooth-glass the sleeping tablets teem.

Ein Treppenhaus

Wenn du nach Dublin kommst, sagte sie damals,
die Adresse hast du ja. Also sitze ich hier
auf der letzten Stufe, unter dem Dach,
im Halbdunkel, ab und zu hallen Schritte
von unten her, klackende Hacken, dann
schlägt eine Tür mit grünem Filz
an die Wand geschrieben: *Komme gleich wieder*,
mit Lipenstift: *Molly war da. Ruf mich an*,
und unter dem abgerissenen Klingeldraht
eine Telefonnummer. Wie viele Jahre lang
wird das noch alles da stehen, die Wörter,
die Wände? Niemand kommt. Und ich frage mich,
wie sie aussah. Nur was mich störte,
das weiß ich noch: ihr elektrisches Zappeln,
der Jodgeruch, das Gelb im Weiß ihrer Augen,
die Puderflecken, das alte Feldbett und später
das Heulen des Teekessels auf dem Herd.
Eine Fremde. Ich rühre mich nicht.
Am liebsten bliebe ich hier, summend,
im Treppenhaus, bis der Bulldozer kommt.

A Staircase

If you're in Dublin, she said that time,
you have the address. So I'm sitting here
on the top stair, under the roof,
in half-light; from time to time I can hear
footsteps below, heels clacking, then
a door slams, silence. Drowsy,
with the help of a lighter, I read
this message scrawled on the wall,
with a green felt pen, near the frame
of the cracked door: *Back very soon*,
with an eye pencil: *Molly was here. Ring me*,
and under the ripped-out doorbell wire
a telephone number. How many more years
are they likely to last, the messages,
the walls? No one comes. And I try to recall
what she looked like. All I remember
is the things I disliked: her electric twitch,
the iodine smell, the yellow in the white of her eyes,
the blotches of powder, the old camp bed and, later,
the howling of her kettle on the stove.
A stranger. I do not stir.
What I'd like best is to stay here, humming
on the staircase, till the bulldozer comes.

Stadtrundfahrt

Da drüben kauert der Schuhputzer,
der keine Schuhe mehr braucht;
denn seine Beine sind verfault
im Fernen Osten vor langer Zeit.

Das ist der Rauch von den Werften.

Dieses Café war früher ganz schwarz
von Hausierern und armen Dichtern.
Spitzel wie Mücken saßen dort
und tranken aus kleinen Tassen Blut.

Hier gibt es weiche Mädchen
gegen harte Devisen.
Das Pflaster ist aufgerissen.
Dort standen damals die Panzer.

Da ist im Sommer immer
der Kaiser spazierengefahren –
Stadtwäldchenallee, heute Gorkij fasor.
Das ist das Zentralkomitee.

Das ist der Rauch von den Schlachthöfen.

Hier ist mein Freund Sandór geboren
vor dem Zweiten Weltkrieg,
in der Beletage,
wo es Tag und Nacht dunkel war.

Siehst du den Rauch?

Diese Brücke war ganz zerstört.
Hier trinken die reichen Dichter Tee
und schimpfen leise,
und dort wird das neue Hilton gebaut.

Sightseeing Tour

Over there the old shoe-shine boy
who can do without shoes,
for his legs rotted away
in the Far East a long time ago.

This is the smoke from the ship-yards.

This café used to be packed
with hawkers and penniless poets.
Informers descended like mosquitoes
and drank blood from little cups.

Here there are soft girls on sale
for hard currency.
The pavement is torn up.
This is where the tanks came in.

Here the Emperor went for his drive
in the summertime, every day –
Stadtwäldchenallee, today Gorkij fasor.
This is the Central Committee.

That is the smoke from the stockyards.

Here my friend Sandór was born
before the Second World War
on the first floor
where the daylight never came in.

Do you see the smoke?

The bridge over there was completely destroyed.
Here the well-to-do poets take their tea
grumbling softly,
and there the new Hilton is going up.

Auf dieser wackligen Parkbank
sitzt manchmal ein alter Mann,
der manchmal die Wahrheit sagt.
Heute ist er nicht da.

Aber der Rauch. Siehst du den Rauch,

den alten Rauch über Budapest?

On this rickety park-bench
an old man can sometimes be seen
who sometimes tells the truth.
He did not show up today.

But the smoke. Do you see the smoke

the old smoke over Budapest?

Kurze Geschichte der Bourgeoisie

Dies war der Augenblick, da wir,
ohne es zu bemerken, fünf Minuten lang
unermeßlich reich waren, großzügig
und elektrisch, gekühlt im Juli,
oder für den Fall daß es November war,
loderte das eingeflogene finnische Holz
in den Renaissancekaminen. Komisch,
alles war da, flog sich ein,
gewissermaßen von selber. Elegant
waren wir, niemand konnte uns leiden.
Wir warfen um uns mit Solokonzerten,
Chips, Orchideen in Cellophan. Wolken,
die Ich sagten. Einmalig!

Überallhin Linienflüge. Selbst unsre Seufzer
gingen auf Scheckkarte. Wie die Rohrspatzen
schimpften wir durcheinander. Jedermann
hatte sein eigenes Unglück unter dem Sitz,
griffbereit. Eigentlich schade drum.
Es war so praktisch. Das Wasser
floß aus den Wasserhähnen wie nichts.
Wißt ihr noch? Einfach betäubt
von unsern winzigen Gefühlen,
aßen wir wenig. Hätten wir nur geahnt,
daß das alles vorbei sein würde
in fünf Minuten, das Roastbeef Wellington
hätte uns anders, ganz anders geschmeckt.

Short History of the Bourgeoisie

That was the moment when, without
noticing it, for five minutes
we were vastly rich, magnificent
and electric, air-conditioned in July,
or, in case it was November,
the flown-in Finnish wood blazed
in Tudor fireplaces. Funny,
it was all there, just flew in
by itself, as it were. Elegant
we were, no one could bear us.
We threw solo concerts around,
chips, orchids in cellophane. Clouds
that said, I. Unique!

Flights everywhere. Even our sighs
went on credit cards. Like sailors
we bandied curses. Each one
had his own misfortune under the seat,
ready to grab at it. A waste, really.
It was so practical. Water
flowed out of taps just like that.
Remember? Simply stunned
by our tiny emotions,
we ate little. If only we'd guessed
that all this would pass
in five minutes, the roast beef Wellington
would have tasted different, quite different.

Die Frösche von Bikini

Bohrende Fragen, Gestichel, Einwände:
Er halte inne, höre zu, aufmerksam,
lasse sich alles gesagt sein.
Die unerfüllbaren Forderungen
seien berechtigt.
Die Vorwürfe zu entkräften
sei er nicht in der Lage.
Nur eines bitte er höflich
nicht zu erwähnen: seine Probleme.

Wenn er das schon höre –
vorgestern erst, auf dem Heimweg,
zwischen Ambulanzen und Betonmischmaschinen,
durch die halb offene Tür einer Telefonzelle:
»Meine Probleme« –
ein quakendes Geräusch aus der Leitung,
oder auch auf Kongressen,
in therapeutischer Absicht:
»Wege zur Selbsterfahrung« –
offenbar gar kein Vergleich
mit anderen Wirbeltieren!

Nein, auf Selbsterfahrung lege er keinen Wert,
und Probleme habe er nicht,
wenigstens keine »eigenen«. Plötzlich,
am Abend, die Übelkeit ohne Ursache,
oder »die Unterdrückung« (im Allgemeinen),
oder die Kreidestriche im Scheinwerferlicht
um einen Fleck auf der Autobahn –
er meine besonders die Kreidestriche – :
was daran Besonderes sei,
vermöge er nicht zu erkennen.
Er müsse auf seine Stimme hören,
das sei alles.

The Frogs of Bikini

Nagging questions, taunting remarks, objections:
He'd stop short, listen attentively,
take stock, take notice.
The demands made upon him, fully justified,
were impossible to comply with;
to refute the recriminations
was out of the question.
Just one thing he'd rather not have mentioned:
his problems.

That sort of talk was getting too much for him –
only the day before yesterday,
on his way home,
amongst cement mixers and ambulances,
through the half-open door of a phone box:
'My personal problems' –
a croaking sound from the earphone,
or at conventions:
'Our path to self-awareness'
(by way of therapy) –
apparently all these animals
were beyond comparison
with other vertebrates!

No, he couldn't care less
about 'being aware',
and as far as he was concerned,
there were no problems to speak of,
at least not 'personal' ones.
Just the sudden attack of nausea,
unaccountably, at night,
the sense of 'repression' (in general),
or else the chalk-marks seen in the glare
of the head-lights round a dark spot
on the motorway: the chalk-marks
gave him food for thought, but to his mind

Gewisse Geister im Schrank, gewisse Adressen –
da draußen, auf einer staubigen Bank
am Mariannenplatz –
ein Pakistani schlurft vorbei –
Ecke Oranienburger würgt etwas,
privat, unbemerkt, erstickt
und steht nicht mehr auf.

Während ich, sagt er,
weil mir nichts anderes übrigbleibt,
horche, auf jene Stimme,
auf daß sie mir sage wohin,
mit wem, wozu – *meine* Stimme,
sagt er, die sich nicht vernehmen läßt,
und das unterscheidet mich von den Irren –,
weint Fräulein Bausch vor dem Spiegel,
magersüchtig, Ansbacher Straße,
vierter Stock, Gartenhaus –
er deute das alles nur an.

Allzu viele Verluste, süße Isolation,
manches, in dem er nicht mehr enthalten sei;
ferner das Alter, die Wiederholungen
und das Geld. Allerdings, behauptet er,
suchte ich, schuftete, schimpfte,
war ehrgeizig wie ein Idiot,
wurde verlassen, verließ,
und wollte alles zerbrechen.

Damals sei der Hunger größer gewesen.
Zerbrochen habe er nichts.
Ob Wiederholungen so etwas Schlechtes seien,
wisse er nicht genau.
Ohne Zwangsvorstellung
gebe es keine Liebe und keine Arbeit.

there was nothing 'personal' about them.
He'd have to listen to the Voice in his head,
that was all.

Certain skeletons in cupboards, certain addresses –
out there, on a dusty bench,
Berlin, Mariannenplatz –
a Pakistani shuffling by –
on the corner of Oranienburger Straße
something will choke, privately, unnoticed,
be quietly throttled, not to get up again.

While I, he says, am harkening,
since I cannot help it, to the Voice,
hoping to be told where to go,
with whom, what for – *my* Voice,
he says, which I cannot hear,
and that's where I differ from the insane –,
Fräulein Bausch will weep
in front of the looking-glass,
anorectic, Ansbacher Straße,
fourth floor, rear wing –
he'd rather not enlarge on the subject.

All too many losses, sweet isolation,
things which have ceased to concern him,
not to mention his age, those recurrences
and money. It is true, he goes on,
I have searched and toiled, insulted everybody,
I was keen like an idiot,
I deserted and was deserted,
I had a mind to smash everything.

I used to be hungrier then. In the event
nothing much got smashed.
Whether recurrence was such a bad thing
he'd now be less sure.
As far as he could see, without *idées fixes*
there would be neither work nor love.

Das ist von mir! ruft Engelchen,
das könne von mir sein! das ist gut! –
bekifft, rote Flecken im Gesicht –,
wirft das Buch weg, schminkt sich,
rauft sich die Haare. Dieser Geruch
aus dem Schlafzimmer,
was ist das? Ammoniak, Gas?
Macht doch die Fenster auf, schnell,
oder schlagt die Tür ein –
merkt denn kein Nachbar was?
Aber die Droysenstraße
liegt völlig verlassen da.

Im August, an entlegenen Stellen,
Schilf und so weiter, Teichlinsen,
höre er, im Licht eines Satelliten,
voller Genugtuung nach Programmschluß
den Fröschen zu. Restbestände.
Diese Vorliebe für alte Häuser,
alte Freiheiten, aussterbende Tiere.
Nichts Besonderes. Aber das Recht
zu quaken und nicht zu quaken –
ihm liege es nun einmal am Herzen,
er bestehe darauf.

Am hellen Nachmittag, anderswo,
verdunkelte Räume. Hier
sind die Vorhänge dick, die Nadeln
glänzen, die Wandtafel mit den Linien
rollt sich im Rauch, es riecht
nach Kampfer. Tiefe Stiche
unter die Haut, natürlich
zum Wohle des Ganzen.
Unblutig lächelt der Akupunkteur.

Oder jene Sitzungen,
auf denen es üblich war,
im Namen der Arbeiterklasse
einander das Nasenbein einzuschlagen,
im übertragenen Sinne natürlich –

That's what I always say! Engelchen cries,
my very words! Exactly!
Stoned, with red spots on his cheeks,
he throws the book away, paints his face,
tears his hair. What is this smell
from the bedroom? Ammonia? Gas?
Quick! Open the windows
or break down the door – where are the neighbours?
Don't they realise what's going on?
Not a soul in sight.
Droysenstraße lies deserted.

Then again, in August, and in remote places,
full of bulrushes, duckweed, etcetera,
he'd listen, after all stations have closed down,
to his heart's content, in the gleam of a satellite,
to the frogs. Residues.
His predilection for old houses,
old liberties, animals on the brink of extinction.
Nothing personal. Just the right
to croak or not to croak –
he'd insist on it.

Somewhere else again, in the afternoon,
a shuttered room. The thick curtains,
the glittering needles, the wall chart
with the twisted lines basking
in the smoke, the camphor fumes.
Deep forays beneath the skin,
all, of course, to the ultimate good
of the patient, and at the last twist
the acupuncturist's bloodless smile.

Or he'd remember the caucus sessions
where it was customary
to bash in each other's nasal bones
in the name of the working class –
figuratively speaking, of course.

Und nun, mein Lieber, haben Sie resigniert?
Nach längerem Nachdenken antwortet er:
Ich bin immer noch da. Und:
Es ist an mir, wie ich glaube,
eine gewisse Beharrlichkeit festzustellen.

Sich Abfinden sei etwas für Optimisten
oder für Tote, etwas Jenseitiges,
komme mithin im Kosmos nicht vor,
sei auch in Friedenau,
dem Stadtviertel, wo er wohne,
eine unbekannte Erscheinung –
ganz im Gegensatz zu Amokläufen,
Tablettenvergiftungen, Psychosen,
kurz, Tathandlungen, Ausbrüchen,
Zerfleischung und Gegenwehr.

Nichts bleibt, wie es ist,
glücklicherweise.
Nicht nur der Frosch,
auch die Froschforschung
kann schließlich zurückblicken
auf Errungenschaften.
Ein ohrenbetäubendes Spektakel.

Auch er werde immer besser,
unwillkürlich, genau wie die Krankheiten,
wie die Zahnkrem, das soziale Netz.
»Auf erweiterter Stufenleiter,«
höre er seine Freunde rufen
von nebenan – »naturwüchsig« –,
und er rufe zurück: Eureka!
Meine Guten, nennt mir doch etwas,
das nicht naturwüchsig wäre.

Vom Laich zur Kaulquappe,
von der Kaulquappe zum Frosch,
vom Frosch zum Fossil.
Ach, was wären wir ohne die erste Evolution,

And now, my dear chap? Have you given in?
After careful reflection he'd answer:
I'm still around. Observing me closely,
you'll find me pig-headed, I believe.

According to his lights, to give in
is a course fit for optimists
and for the dead, something transcendent
in short, not to be found in our universe,
let alone in Friedenau, his own
quarter of Berlin – where on the other hand
all sorts of rash acts abound,
family murders, psychoses,
sleeping pill suicides, i.e. mayhem,
havoc and self-defence.

Nothing, fortunately,
remains as it is.
Not only the frogs can look back
on splendid achievements.
Frog ethology, too,
has made great strides.
Altogether a deafening show.

He himself, would advance, as well,
involuntarily, just like the diseases
around him, like toothpaste
and social security, on a higher scale.
'Naturally,' his friends would shout
from next door, and he'd call back:
'Eureka! My dear fellows, can you think
of anything outside of Nature?

From spawn to tadpole,
from tadpole to frog,
from frog to fossil.
Where would we be without the first,

und die zweite, was wäre sie ohne uns!
Ohne quak wäre quak nicht quak,
und umgekehrt. Wohin er auch höre,
keine Stimme, nur
der wunderbare Gesang der Mutanten.

Ohrenbetäubend und immer neu
ineinander verbissen
diese subtilen Nahrungsketten,
und weich und stumm
ineinander verschlungen
die grauen Lappen der Rinde.

»Über einige strukturelle Eigentümlichkeiten
des sozialen Verhaltens bei *rana rana*«:
All die Fossilien im Sediment
unseres Gehirns rühren sich,
zappeln, elektrisieren uns:
die Erste, die Zweite, die Dritte Natur,
etc. (N_1, N_2, N_3,…N_n).

Selbst jene Wolke dort, die er,
vor sich hinmurmelnd, betrachte,
voller Genugtuung, habe sich,
während er murmle, verändert,
naturwüchsig, wattig, fern,
wie gewisse Wörter,
im Aussterben begriffen,
die ihm teuer seien, wie »Wollust«,
»Verlangen«, »Begierde« – Zustände,
instabil wie das Positron,
doch längst nicht so gut erforscht.

Auch jenes wachsverklebte Bett,
jenes Zimmer, schwarz gestreift
vom Ruß der Kerzen, hat eine Adresse;
ihr blakendes Licht,
die achtlos wechselnden Tageszeiten –
ich werde das Haus nicht wiederfinden.

and where would the second evolution
end up without us? Croak
would hardly be croak without croak,
and vice versa. Whichever way
he'd cock his ear, no voice to be heard,
save the wondrous song of the mutants.

Deafening and forever novel
the subtle food-chains
locking their teeth,
and soft and silently twisting
the grey folds of the cortex.

'On some structural peculiarities
in the social behaviour of *rana rana*':
All those fossils in the sediment of our brain
begin to quiver, to quake, to electrify us:
First Nature, Second Nature, Third,
etcetera (N_1, N_2, N_3,...N_n).

Even the cloud over there,
which he'd contemplate to his heart's content,
talking softly to himself, would change,
'naturally', fuzzily, in the distance
just like certain words, on the brink
of extinction, words dear to him,
like 'Longing', 'Desire', 'Lust',
standing for states as shortlived
as the position, though
far less well-studied by science.

The bed that used to be plastered
with wax droppings, the room darkly striped
by the soot of candles, must have an address
somewhere, their fluttering light,
the times of the day passing unnoticed –
I shall not find the door again.

Oder Bikini. Er denke oft an Bikini.
Alles sei wieder da,
dreißig Jahre nach der Apokalypse,
»auf erweiterter Stufenleiter«.
Laubfrösche, taufrisch,
unaufhaltsam. Ein Klettern sei das,
eine Akrobatik, sogar das Wetter
mache Fortschritte. Das Weiß
der Strände, menschenleer –

Wie am gestirnten Himmel über uns
die harte Strahlung, der Helium-Flash,
die hemmungslose Verschwendung,
so auch hienieden. Das Glück –
er wage es kaum, das Wort
in den Mund zu nehmen –, das Glück,
selten, plötzlich, unzweifelhaft
(je nach Chromosomensatz, Klassenlage,
Hormonspiegel, Uhrzeit),
sei vielleicht das letzte Verbrechen.

Der Mann, der am Sonntag verzweifeln muß,
weil am Sonntag das Telefonieren billiger ist,
der Mann, der an den Worten seiner Frau,
einer Fremden hängt, wie an einem Strick,
dieser Mann sei er. Du
hättest nicht zu betteln, ich
hätte dich nicht zu schlagen, wir
hätten einander nicht zu verlieren brauchen –
das alles am Telefon, das alles am Sonntag,
und anderen Leuten, das wisse er wohl,
schiene dieser Abgrund vielleicht
nur ein paar Zentimeter tief –

Gleich bin ich fertig; an meinem Leumund
liegt mir nichts; mein Abschreiber,
mein Polyp, mein Blutegel, Professor Fels,
der »über mich arbeitet« – einer von denen –,
siehe, er langweilt sich schon.

Or else Bikini. He'd find himself often
thinking of it. Things in Bikini
were back to normal, everything had returned,
thirty years after the apocalypse,
'on a higher scale'. Tree frogs,
fresh as daisies, scrambling up the scale
to the top, progressively,
like acrobats. There's no stopping them.
Even the weather will improve in time.
The beaches white, untouched by human feet.

Dissipation, extravagance, just like above us
the starry skies, full of hard radiation,
of helium-flashes, life here below
goes on lavishly. Bliss –
he'd hardly dare utter the word –,
bliss, rare, sudden, indubitable
(determined, naturally, by chromosome sets,
class, hormone levels, and the time of the day)
may be the ultimate crime.

The man who's got to shelve his despair
until Sunday, because it is cheaper
to call long distance on Sundays,
the man who hangs on the lips of his woman,
a stranger's lips, as on a rope,
that's me, he shouts. For no earthly reason
you begged me, I beat you, we lost each other –
all this on the telephone, on a Sunday –
and as he was well aware, this abyss
would have seemed, to the rest of the world,
rather shallow –

Don't worry, I shall be done presently,
I do not care about my good name;
my scribe, my parasite, my leech,
Professor Fels, who is 'working on me',
look, he must be bored by now with his thesis.

Im übrigen bin ich Zuschauer. Ja,
ich schaue zu. Diese Pflichtübungen,
Maiandachten und Prozessionen,
behauptet er, habe er satt. Bis zum Hals
in löchrigen Schnürstiefeln
eine Halde von alten Schuhen zu überqueren
mit durchgelaufenen Sohlen –
wenn das der Neue Mensch sei,
dann lieber nicht.

Der hat leicht reden.
Und wie stehts mit dem Geld?

Wohnungen, Wagen, Steuerbescheide:
ja, meine Liebste, es stimmt,
ich habe manchmal daran gedacht,
an die Sicherheit, daß ich nicht lache,
wie der Laubfrosch im Glas.
Aber sie beruhigt mich nicht,
die Sicherheit, sie macht Angst.
Daher, glaub mir, kommt meine Ruhe nicht.
Sie nickt verächtlich und geht,
die eine, die mit den hellen Augen,
aber die andere, die keine Furcht hat
und klüger ist, sie wird mir glauben.
Und es ist wahr, daß ich niemanden finde,
der zu beneiden wäre.

Wahr ist (*stockend; niedergeschlagen*),
daß ich den Schmerz nicht verstehen kann
in eurem Namen. Teilnahmslos
bin ich nicht, sondern geständig.
(*Matt. Zu sich selber.*) Merkwürdig,
was einem alles sympathisch wird mit der Zeit.
Was alles von selber verschwindet.
Was einen dauert. (*Pause. Drohend.*)
Aber ich kann auch anders.
Laßt mir Herrn Dr. Benn in Ruhe!
Belle-Alliance-Straße, alle Kassen.

Anyway, I'm just an onlooker,
standing by, peering. All those marches,
devotions and exercises he claims to be sick of.
If you have to cross a heap of old shoes,
on wornout soles, up to the neck
in battered lace-boots
in order to become a New Man –
why, he'd rather not.

Oh well, it is easy for you to talk!
What about your bank account?

It is perfectly true, my dear girl,
I too, at times, have been thinking
of cars, houses, tax returns,
of putting an end to my worries,
of security, like a frog in his jar.
What a joke! But in the event,
it gave me no peace, security,
it worried me stiff. No, my calm,
believe me, is of another kind.
She will give me a nod of scorn
and turn away, the bright-eyed girl,
but the other one who is fearless
and wise, she will believe me.
And it is true that I never found
any man I could envy.

It is true (*slight stammer, dejected look*)
that I cannot understand pain
on your behalf. It is not
as if I did not care. I plead guilty.
(*Tired voice. To himself.*) Extraordinary,
the things one comes to sympathise with
in the long run. The things that vanish.
The things one regrets. (*Pause. Menacing tone.*)
But I am not a sucker! And I ask you
to leave Dr Benn alone.
He treated no private patients,

Seine Patienten jedenfalls
haben sich nie über ihn beklagt.

(*Leise.*) Bis zu einem gewissen Grad
mach ich gemeinsame Sache mit euch.
Aber wir wollen nicht übertreiben.
(*Sehr bestimmt.*) Meine Ruhe,
soweit davon die Rede sein kann,
ist nicht terroristisch. (*Brüsk.*)
Was, Lichtblicke? Oh,
Lichtblicke gibt es genug. Nur da nicht,
wo ihr sie sucht, oder ich.
Utopien? Gewiß, aber wo?
Wir sehen sie nicht. Wir fühlen sie nur
wie das Messer im Rücken.

Unter diesen Umständen müsse er sich
zuweilen der Stimme enthalten.
Er höre die Stecknadeln fallen,
während die Frösche sich heiser schrien
in den Bombenkratern des Fortschritts,
wo der Regen neue Tümpel bildet,
naturwüchsig: N_n sive deus.
Nicht ohne Zuversicht erwarte er
die Abschaffung unsrer Abschaffungen.
Ein schöner Septembertag.
Klammer zu. Ende der Abschweifung.

Seine Lieblingsdroge
sei die Aufmerksamkeit.
Auf die tägliche Prise
von ideologischem Kokain
könne er notfalls verzichten;
und wenn es schon nicht abgehe ohne Moral –
die seine bestehe darin,
nicht zu ermüden. Aufmerksam
wie seine Freundin beim Schminken,
wie der Moskito im Schlafzimmer,
wie der Spitzel vor jedermanns Haus,

and no one who came to him
ever complained.

(*Softly*.) Up to a point I cast in my lot
with yours. Solidarity by all means.
But let's not exaggerate.
(*Pointedly*.) My calm, as far as it goes,
is not based on terror. (*Brusquely*.)
What? Silver linings? Oh,
there's plenty of them. Not,
of course, where you or I
would look for them. Utopias?
Certainly. But where are they?
Out of sight. We can only feel them
like a knife sticking in our back.

Under these circumstances
every now and then he'd have to abstain.
He could hear a pin falling
while the frogs shout themselves hoarse
in the bomb craters of progress,
where the rain will form ever new ponds,
naturally: N_n *sive deus*.
He'd look forward, hopefully,
to the aboliton of our abolitions.
A marvellous day in September.
Parenthesis closed. End of digression.

His favourite drug, he maintains,
is alertness, the daily dose
of ideological cocaine
he'd just as well do without;
and if some sort of morals are indispensable,
as they say, well, his own would forbid him
to flag. Attentively,
like his girlfriend painting her lips,
like the mosquito hovering in the bedroom,
like the plain-clothes man at the front door,
like the frog who will jump into the pond

wie der Frosch, der ins Wasser springt
bei der geringsten Bewegung,
(und aus ähnlichen Gründen)
betrachte er alles, was der Fall sei.
Seine fünfundzwanzig Sinne reichten hin,
ein Gehirn zu beschäftigen.

Nebenan Kirchenlieder,
gesungen von ältlichen Adventisten.
Friedenau. Wolkenfelder.
Die Massaker, zu denen »es kommt«.
»Historisch«. Sag mir doch etwas,
das nicht »historisch« wäre.
Er murmelt das alles vor sich hin, zerstreut,
abgelenkt von den hundertzwölftausend Farben,
die sein Auge unterscheiden kann.

Einmal, Richtung Bodensee, an der Ausfahrt,
war etwas Weiches zu sehen,
glitzernd im Scheinwerferlicht.
Rettungsfahrzeuge, Männer mit Stangen,
mit Netzen. Ein schwaches Geräusch
unter den Rädern, schlürfend, feucht,
übertönt im Fond von der Kadenz,
Mozart, Klavierkonzert, zweiter Satz –
diese ländliche Gegend,
Flach- und Zwischenmoor,
für die Frösche auf ihrer Wanderung
war sie Bikini.

Da ich aber beschlossen habe,
unauffällig zu sein,
bescheiden, maßvoll und höflich,
und da es nicht üblich ist,
einander laut zu verfluchen,
werde ich meinen Zettel
nicht auseinanderfalten,
die Liste der Ungeheuer
in winziger Schrift, wie das Vaterunser,

at the slightest sign of trouble
(and for similar reasons)
he'd have an eye on everything that transpires.
His twenty-five senses were quite sufficient
to keep his brain busy.

Hymns from next door,
sung by elderly adventists.
Herds of clouds passing by
over Berlin-Friedenau.
The massacres which 'result',
'historically'. Tell me something
that would be outside of History.
He's absent-minded, he mumbles distracted
by the hundred and twelve thousand shades of colour
which his eye can discern.

Once, on the way to Lake Constance,
on the motorway exit, something soft
was to be seen, shining
in the glare of the head-lights.
Emergency patrols, men
brandishing poles and nets.
There was a soft swish underneath the wheels,
something moist, drowned
by the notes of the cadence, Mozart,
piano concerto, second movement –
this part of the country,
marshlands, moors,
for the frogs on their last migration
it was Bikini.

Since I have decided, once and for all,
to be inconspicuous,
modest, well-tempered and civil,
and since it is not good form
to curse one another shrilly,
I shall not unfold at present
my piece of paper, my list

in einen Kirschkern geritzt, –
auch weil der Zettel, entfaltet,
uns alle bedecken würde.

Verschwendete Flüche tragen nicht weit.
Ich spare, ich kratze zusammen
das, was ich habe, ich laure,
bis er die Glastür aufstößt
mit seinem glänzenden weißen Gesicht,
der Pharisäer, der ewiglich
bessere Mensch, die Sau
mit dem guten Gewissen:
ihm werfe ich meinem Fluch
vor den Bauch, meine Bombe.

Wer ist hier der Pharisäer?
Wie alt sind Sie überhaupt?
Meinen Sie etwa mich?
Sind Sie verrückt,
einfach hier anzurufen
am Sonntagnachmittag?

Was soll das heißen, Ungeheuer?
Von jetzt an nehme ich jedes Wort,
das Sie sagen, auf Band.

Das alles ist schon eine Weile her.
Hier, weit draußen, Altbau,
Blick auf den Garten,
sind keine Frösche zu hören.
Ich schaue zu. Ich merke, was los ist.
Diese Wolke dort drüben stirbt
vollkommen still. Ich habe verlernt
zu sagen: »Im Gegenteil«.
Hier ist nichts los. Ich warte,
ruhig. Irgendwo kämpfen die Feinde,
nach wie vor, die alten Feinde,
immer ähnlicher einer dem andern,
gleichgültiger, ferner,
immer woanders.

of monsters, drawn up in minute script
like the Lord's Prayer engraved
onto a cherry-stone –
if only because my piece of paper,
unfolded, would cover us all.

Spent curses will not carry far.
I save them, I scrape together
all I have, I lurk,
until he pushes the glass-door open,
he with the shiny white face,
the Pharisee, the eternal do-gooder,
the self-righteous pig.
Then I will thrust my curse,
my bomb, in his lap.

What do you mean by Pharisee?
Are you of age? Why
are you looking at me?
Are you mad, to ring me up,
a perfect stranger,
on a Sunday afternoon?

Looking for monsters, here
of all places! From now on
all you say will be taped!

In the meantime, out here,
where the houses are old and worn,
and the back-gardens overgrown,
no frogs are in evidence.
I am looking on, I have an eye
on everything that goes on.
The cloud over there dies
in perfect stillness. I've given up
saying: 'On the contrary'.
Nothing much is going on.
I wait, calmly. Somewhere else
there are enemies fighting,

Aber ich bin doch hier,
ich hänge an euch, ich brüte doch
über euerm Brüten. Im toten Winkel,
hinter den ringsum aufgetürmten,
undurchschaubaren, sperrigen Möbeln
atmet es, eingepreßt –
verstellt euch nicht! Ihr hört es
so gut wie ich: ein, aus,
ein, aus – dieser Blasebalg,
den wir nicht sehen können –,
ich kann ihn nicht sehen,
wie er da liegt im Staub und regelmäßig,
regelmäßig, regelmäßig ächzt, ledern
keucht –, davon, davon
erzähle ich euch, dumpf und regelmäßig.

Ich will nicht, daß ihr ihn tauft,
bezeichnet, diskutiert, diesen Balg.
Horcht lieber, mir zuliebe,
ich bitte euch, oder lacht.

Lacht nur! Das macht doch nichts.
Zeit vergeht. Wenn ihr wollt,
halten wir einander den Mund zu,
wenn euch das lieber ist, auch die Ohren –
oder ihr schnupft, kaut, raucht, spritzt,
ich mache mit, ich bin dabei,
wir haben Zeit, macht das Licht an,
wer baden will, badet,
ich sage nicht: »Im Gegenteil«,
im Gegenteil! Werft die Kleider weg,
saugt aneinander
wer nicht will, hat schon,
feuchtet euch an,
jeder nach seinen Bedürfnissen,
fünf Minuten vor zwölf.

the old enemies, resembling each other
more and more in the process,
more and more indifferent and remote,
somewhere else.

But I am still here, I hold forth,
I cling to you, I brood
over your broodings. In the dead angle
behind the unwieldy, impenetrable
furniture towering all around me
I can hear something breathing,
a wheeze – don't pretend
that you cannot hear it:
in, out, in, out, a pair of bellows
out of sight. I cannot see it.
It's crouching there in the dust
and evenly, evenly, evenly groaning,
leathery, gasping,
that's it, that's what I'm telling you
dully and even.

I do not want you to name it,
to label it, to discuss it,
this pair of bellows over there
in the corner. Just listen,
for my sake, for your sake,
I beseech you, listen to it or laugh.
Laugh if you like. It does not matter.
Time passes. If you will,
we might gag each other,
or, if you prefer, plug our ears.

Or you could snuff, chew, smoke, shoot,
I am with you, I do as you do
there is plenty of time,
put on the lights, if you will,
he who wants a bath, let him take it,
I don't say: 'On the contrary',
on the contrary! Throw off your clothes,

Das könne lange dauern.
Er sei kein Prophet,
über manches rede er nicht,
er deute nur an, warte, und seine Stimme
lasse er nur deshalb erschallen,
weil sonst keine Stimme zu hören sei,
keine Angst, keine Tränen,
er sei ja da, er bleibe.

Ich bleibe, sagt er,
wir sagen einander ins Ohr,
was wir gewollt hätten,
wenn wir nicht dem Warten verfallen wären,
dem atemlosen selbstsüchtigen Horchen
auf unsern Atemzug, wie er dort hinten
rassle, im toten Winkel, innen
rassle, regelmäßig
rassle.

suck one another,
take it or leave it, cream,
to everyone according to his needs,
it is five to twelve.

This sort of thing might go on
for quite some time.
He'd not qualify as a prophet.
There were things he'd rather not talk about.
He'd just drop a hint every now and then,
he'd wait, and his voice would resound
only because there was no other voice
to be heard, no panic, no tears.
He was here to stay.

I am here to stay, he says,
let's whisper in one another's ear
what we might have wanted to do
if we'd not succumbed to the waiting,
to our breathless, selfish harkening
to our very own breath,
to the rattle over there
rattling evenly,
in the dead angle,
the rattle within.

Automat

Er zieht Zigaretten
für ein paar Mark Zigaretten

Er zieht den Krebs
er zieht die Apartheid
er zieht ein paar entfernte Massaker

Er zieht und zieht
doch indem er zieht
verschwindet alles was er zieht

Auch die Zigaretten verschwinden

Er blickt den Automaten an
Er sieht sich selber
Für einen Augenblick
sieht er aus wie ein Mensch

Dann verschwindet er wieder
Mit einem Klacks
fallen die Zigaretten

Er ist verschwunden
Es war nur ein Augenblick
Es war eine Art von Glück

Er ist verschwunden
Unter dem was er gezogen hat
liegt er begraben

Vending Machine

He puts four dimes into the slot
he gets himself some cigarettes

He gets cancer
he gets apartheid
he gets a couple of far-away massacres

He gets more and more
for his four dimes
but for a moment all the things disappear

Even the cigarettes

He looks at the vending machine
He sees himself
For a fleeting moment
he almost looks like a man

Then very soon he is gone again
with a little click
there are his cigarettes

He has disappeared
it was just a fleeting moment
some kind of sudden bliss

He has disappeared
he is gone
buried under all the stuff he got
for his four dimes

Die Glasglocke

Besonders morgens ist, in den Gewächshäusern,
schräg gegenüber, wo Gurken gedeihen,
ohne Rücksicht auf Mord und Totschlag,
ich gähne freudig, alles in Ordnung.
Aus meinem Hahn, dessen kaltes Email
KALT sagt, schwarz auf weiß, fließt wie immer
das Wasser warm. Der Trödler schräg gegenüber
zieht seinen Rolladen hoch, donnernd.
Ich sehe Leute, die kehren, backen,
nageln, zählen, waschen und schreiben.
Ich schreibe, ordentlich. Möbelpacker
sind da, rollschuhfahrende Kinder. Warum
so ordentlich? so gewaltlos? als wäre
nichts der Fall? Am offenen Fenster
stimmt jemand ein Klavier, ich kann nur
seine Hände sehen, wie nackt sie sind
und wie weich! Ein Kühlschrank beginnt
zu summen, Züge sind pünktlich, es dreht sich
unter der glasigen Haube des Zählers
lautlos ein Ring, in der Morgensonne
glitzernd. Ein Mann steht, winzig
und hellblau, schräg gegenüber, hoch
auf dem Dach, er wippt, er bückt sich,
er klopft an das verzinkte Blech, ich sehe
ihn klopfen, aber ich höre nichts.
Ein scheckiger Frieden dehnt sich, weich
und winzig, am Vormittag, halb betäubt
von der Sonne, in einer alltäglichen Trance,
und streckt sich gelb, wie die Katze
auf dem Zementsack, schräg gegenüber.

The Bell Jar

In the mornings especially, in the greenhouses
across the road, where cucumbers thrive,
regardless of assault and murder,
I yawn happily, everything is normal.
From my tap, whose cold enamel
says COLD, in bold letters, as usual the water
runs warm. The junk merchant across the road
with a thundering noise, raises his shutter.
I see people who sweep, bake,
nail, count, wash and write.
I write, normally. Furniture removers
are here, roller-skating children. Why
so normal? So unviolent? as though
nothing were wrong? At the open window
someone tunes a piano. I can see
only his hands, how naked they are,
and how soft! A refrigerator begins
to hum, trains are on time, under
the meter's glass cover a disk
revolves without a sound and glitters
in the morning sunshine. A man, tiny
and pale blue, across the road,
stands high up on the roof, he teeters, he bends down,
he taps the galvanised sheeting, I see
him tap, but I hear nothing.
A mottled quiet spreads out, tiny
and soft, into the morning, half dazed
by the sun, in an everyday trance,
and yellowly stretches, like the cat
on that bag of cement, across the road.

Nicht Zutreffendes streichen

Was deine Stimme so flach macht
so dünn und so blechern
das ist die Angst
etwas Falsches zu sagen

oder immer dasselbe
oder das zu sagen was alle sagen
oder etwas Unwichtiges
oder Wehrloses
oder etwas das mißverstanden werden könnte
oder den falschen Leuten gefiele
oder etwas Reaktionäres
oder etwas Kitschiges
oder etwas Dummes
oder etwas schon Dagewesenes
etwas Altes

Hast du es denn nicht satt
aus lauter Angst
aus lauter Angst vor der Angst
etwas Falsches zu sagen

immer das Falsche zu sagen?

Delete the Inapplicable

What makes your voice so flat
so thin and tinny
is your fear
of saying the wrong thing

or always the same thing
or saying what everyone says
or saying something unimportant
or something vulnerable
or something that could be misunderstood
or that could please the wrong people
or something reactionary
or something in bad taste
or something stupid
or something old hat
something stale

Aren't you tired of it –
only for fear
only for fear of the fear
of saying the wrong thing

saying the wrong thing always?

Der Kamm

Sie blenden mich. Sie sind schön im Vorübergehn.
Ich bewundere Sie, im Schnee, an der Haltestelle,
wie Sie sich morgens geschmückt haben, militant
und mit letzter Kraft. Eine, die nicht hinkt,
die sich nicht bücken will nach dem Groschen
im Schnee, die ihre Gebrechen verbirgt, unheilbar,
wie ich. Und diesen Kamm, der in Ihrem Haar glänzt.
Flammendes Schildpatt. Allerdings, dem
fehlen auch ein paar Zähne. – Ach bewundern,
das kann ein jeder sagen. – Verzeihen Sie,
ich meine nur das, was niemand braucht,
was keinerlei Eindruck an Ihnen macht:
den Zehennagel, der langsam gedeiht, das Haar,
die feuchte, hinfällige Haut; kleine Ströme,
nervöse Absonderungen, vorübergehend
wie Ihre Seele, die nicht geschickt ist,
mürbe, von Tabletten zerfressen, erbsenklein,
verloren in Ihrem Brustkorb. Ja, natürlich,
wir müssen fort, haben keine Zeit. Ich weiß.
Was wollte ich sagen? Ja. Weinen Sie weiter.
Ihr Kamm! – Wie bitte? – Sie haben ihn
fallenlassen. Dort auf dem Pflaster liegt er,
wo vorhin der Schnee war, geheimnisvoll
und gewöhnlich. Bald wird er zertreten sein.
Das ist unvermeidlich. Das kann ein jeder sagen.
Ich mache keinerlei Eindruck. Ich sehe ihn
in der Sonne glänzen. Hören Sie nicht auf mich.
Meine Wörter bücken sich nicht. Sie sind
nicht dazu da, etwas aufzuheben. Sie sind da,
eine Weile lang. Es kann sie ein jeder sagen.

The Comb

You dazzle me. You are beautiful in passing.
I admire you, in snow, at the bus stop,
how you've adorned yourself in the morning, militant
and with a last effort. One who does not limp,
who refuses to stoop for the penny
dropped into snow, who conceals her ailments, incurable
as I am. And this comb that shines in your hair.
Blazing tortoiseshell. True enough, it too
lacks a few teeth. Oh, admire –
anyone can say that. – Forgive me,
I mean only that which nobody needs,
that about you which makes no impression at all:
the toenail that slowly thrives, the hair,
the moist, perishable skin; little currents,
nervous secretions, ephemeral
as your soul that's devoid of skill,
brittle, riddled with pills, tiny as a pea,
lost in your ribcage. Yes, of course,
we must move on, have no time. I know.
What did I want to say? Yes. Don't stop crying.
Your comb! – Pardon? – You've
dropped it. There it lies, on the pavement,
where the snow was a moment ago, mysterious
and commonplace. Soon it will snap, trodden on.
That can't be helped. Anyone can say that.
I make no impression at all. I see it
gleam in the sun. Don't listen to me.
My words don't bend down. They're not here
for picking up things. They are here,
for a while. Anyone can say them.

Die Kleider

Da liegen sie, still und katzenhaft
in der Sonne, nachmittags,
deine Kleider, ausgebeult,
traumlos, wie ein Zufall.
Sie riechen nach dir, schwach,
sehen dir beinah ähnlich.
Deinen Schmutz überliefern sie,
deine schlechten Gewohnheiten,
die Spur deiner Ellenbogen.
Sie haben Zeit, atmen nicht,
sind übrig, schlaff, voller Knöpfe,
Eigenschaften und Flecken.
In der Hand eines Polizisten,
einer Schneiderin, eines Archäologen
gäben sie ihre Nähte preis,
ihre nichtigen Geheimnisse.
Aber wo du bist, ob du leidest,
was du mir immer hast sagen wollen
und nie gesagt hast,
ob du wiederkommst, ob das,
was geschah, aus Liebe geschah
oder aus Not oder Vergeßlichkeit,
und warum dies alles so,
wie es gekommen ist,
gekommen ist,
als es ums nackte Leben ging,
ob du tot bist, oder ob
du dir nur die Haare wäschst,
das sagen sie nicht.

Clothes

Here they lie, still and cat-like
in the sun, in the afternoon,
your clothes, baggy,
undreaming, as if by chance.
They smell of you, faintly,
they almost take after you,
give away your dirt,
your bad habits,
the trace of your elbows.
They take their time, don't breathe,
are left over, limp, full of buttons,
properties, stains.
In the hands of a policeman,
a dressmaker, an archaeologist
they would reveal their seams,
their idle secrets. But where you are,
whether you suffer, what
you had always wanted to tell me
and never did, whether
what happened has happened
for love's sake or from need
or from negligence, and why
all this has come about as it did
when it was a question
of saving our skin,
whether you are dead by now
or have gone to wash your hair,
they do not tell.

Besuch bei Ingres

Heute hätte er für das ZK gemalt, oder für die Paramount,
je nachdem. Aber damals schwitzten die Gangster noch
unter dem Hermelin, und die Hochstapler ließen sich krönen.
Also her mit Insignien, Perlen und Pfauenfedern.

Wir treffen den Künstler sinnend an. Er hat sich ausgestopft
mit »gewählten Gedanken und edlen Leidenschaften«.
Eine mühsame Sache. Teure Sesselchen, Erstes Empire oder Zweites,
je nachdem. Weiches Kinn, weiche Hände, »Griechentum in der
    Seele«.

Sechzig Jahre lang diese kalte Gier, jeder Zoll ein Könner,
bis es erreicht war: die Rosette im Knopfloch, der Ruhm.

Diese Frauen, die sich vor ihm auf dem Marmor winden
wie Robben aus Hefeteig: zwischen Daumen und Zeigefinger
die Brüste gemessen, die Oberfläche studiert wie Plüsch,
Tüll, Spiegeltaft, die Feuchtigkeit in den Augenwinkeln
zwölfmal lasiert wie Gelatine, das Inkarnat glatt
und narkotisch, besser als Kodak: ausgestellt
in der École des Beaux-Arts, eine käufliche Ewigkeit.

Wozu das Ganze? Wozu das Blech der Orden,
der fanatische Fleiß, die vergoldeten Adler aus Gips?

Merkwürdig schwammig sieht er mit achtzig aus,
erschöpft, den Zylinderhut in der linken Hand.
»Es war alles umsonst.« Aber aber, verehrter Meister!
Was soll denn der Rahmenmacher, der Glaser von Ihnen denken,
die treue Köchin, der Leichenwäscher? Einzige Antwort:

Er seufzt. Hoch über den Wolken, onirisch, die Finger der Thetis,
die sich wie Würmer ringeln auf Jupiters schwarzem Bart.
Widerwillig werfen wir einen letzten Blick
auf den Künstler – wie kurz seine Beine sind! –
und verlassen auf Zehenspitzen das Atelier.

Visiting Ingres

Today he'd be painting for the Central Committee, or Paramount,
it all depends. But at that time a gangster still sweated
under his ermine, and the con-men had themselves crowned.
So let's have them, the insignia, pearls, the peacock feathers.

We find the artist pensive. He has stuffed himself
with 'choice ideas and noble passions'.
A laborious business. Expensive small armchairs, First or Second
    Empire,
it all depends. Soft chin, soft hands, 'Hellas in his soul'.

For sixty years this cold greed, every inch a craftsman,
till he's achieved it: fame, the rosette in his buttonhole.

These women, writhing in front of him on the marble
like seals made of risen dough: between thumb and forefinger
the breasts measured, the surface studied like plush,
tulle, glossy taffeta, the moisture in the corner of their eyes
glazed twelve times over like gelatine, the flesh colour smooth
and narcotic, better than Kodak: exhibited
in the École des Beaux-Arts, a venal eternity.

What's it all for? What for the tin of his decorations,
the fanatical industry, the gilt plaster eagles?

Curiously bloated he looks at eighty,
worn out, with that top hat in his left hand.
'It was all for nothing'. How can you say that, most honoured Maître!
What will the frame-maker think of you, the glazier?
your faithful cook, the undertaker? His only answer:

A sigh. Far above the clouds, oniric, the fingers of Thetis
that squirm like worms on Jupiter's black beard.
Reluctantly we take a last brief look
at the artist – how short his legs are! –
and tiptoe out of the studio.

Ein Traum

Ich bin auf der Flucht. Ich habe meine Schuhe verloren.
Kirschbäume blühen hinter einem verlassenen Haus.
Der Zaun ist zerbrochen. Meine Füße sind staubig, wund.
Ich sitze im Gras, schlafe ein. Durch das offene Fenster
blicke ich in ein Zimmer, das weiß und kühl ist. Im Traum
sehe ich einen alten Mann barfuß vor einer Leinwand stehen.
Er kehrt mir den Rücken zu. Leicht gebückt
tanzelt er in der Morgensonne und setzt
mit winzigen Strichen rasch ein paar Schuhe hin,
zwinkernd. Wie leicht das geht! Der Geruch
der Farbe ist stechend und fett, und im schrägen Licht
funkelt der nasse Pinsel, jedes einzelne Haar.
Die Zeit vergeht. Weich und rehbraun malt er
die beiden Stiefelchen nebeneinander, etwas versetzt,
in das weiche Gras. Ich rieche das Leder. Die Schlaufen,
die Zungen glänzen matt, ich kann die Haken zählen,
die eisernen Ösen. Außer im Kopf des Malers
und auf seinem Bild sind keine Schuhe da.
Von der Straße her höre ich Leute murmeln,
Hundegebell, Lärm. War das nicht ein Schuß?
Warum tust du das, rufe ich im Traum, was du tust?
Hast du kein Leder? – Er rührt sich nicht. – Ja.
sie sind schön, aber was heißt schön? Bekommst du
Geld dafür? – Ich glaube, er lacht. – Außerdem
sind sie alt und abgetragen. – Er stellt sich taub,
wirft einen Blick auf das Bild, zuckt die Achseln
und geht. Die Stiefelchen stehen warm,
wie zwei schlafende Hasen, im Gras.

A Dream

I am on the run. I have lost my shoes.
Cherry trees in bloom behind a deserted house.
Broken fences. My feet are dusty and sore.
I rest in the grass and go to sleep. Through the open window
I peer into a whitewashed, cool room. In my dream
I see an old man standing barefoot in front of a canvas.
He is turning his back on me. Slightly stooping
he prances in the morning sun and deftly does
with tiny dashes a pair of shoes, blinking.
The ease of it! And the smell of paint!
pungent, oily, the wet brush glittering
in a slanting shaft of light, every single hair.
Time passes. Two little lace-up boots he paints,
soft and reddish brown, side by side, a bit staggered,
onto the soft grass. I smell their leather. I see
the dull sheen of the tongues. I can count
the hooks and the iron eyes. Except in the painter's mind
and on his canvas no shoes are in evidence.
I hear people murmuring on the road outside,
dogs barking, noise. Was there a shot?
Why do you do what you do? I ask in my dream.
Have you no leather? – He does not move. – Beautiful,
yes, they are beautiful, but what does that mean?
Does it pay? – He is laughing now, I believe. – Besides,
they are old and worn. – He ignores what I say,
he glances at the picture, he shrugs
and goes away. The lace-up boots stand small,
warm, like two sleeping hares, in the grass.

MUSIC OF THE FUTURE
ZUKUNFTSMUSIK

(1991)

Gillis van Coninxloo, Landschaft.
Holz, 64 x 119 cm

Die Verstoßung der Hagar,
scheußliche Scheidungsgeschichte,
Genesis 20, 21,
was daran heilig sein soll,
weiß der Himmel.

Aber der Faltenwurf,
aber das Wasser,
das unter der Brücke schäumt,
die spielenden Hunde, die Burg
auf dem Fels in der Ferne,
die Frau in der roten Schürze,
die auf dem Wasen die Wäsche auslegt
zum Bleichen, und der Fischer
in seinem Bretterhaus am Teich,
winzig – es sieht ganz so aus,
als wäre er eingeschlafen,
wie die Eule hoch im Geäst.

Dort, wo ich bin,
angelt niemand, kein Reiher
kreischt, die blaue Burg
ist keine blaue Burg, der Kampf
im Zimmer wirft keine Falten.

Eine Prise Pulver, in Öl gelöst,
das ist alles, auf einem Brett.
Es ist nicht da, was ich sehe,
es fehlt. Ein Trug der Augen.
Ich will betrogen sein
und betrügen.
Was daran heilig sein soll,
weiß der Himmel.
Unter der Brücke schäumen,
frischer als Wasser,
Grünspan, Bleiweiß und Malachit.

Gillis van Conninxloo, Landscape. Panel, 65 x 119cm

Hagar repudiated,
Genesis 20, 21,
an abominable divorce story,
supposed to be sacred,
Heaven knows why.

But then the folds of the robe,
the water foaming
beneath the bridge,
the playful hounds, the castle
on the rock in the distance,
the woman with the red apron
spreading her linen to bleach
in the meadow, and in his shed
the fisherman by the pond,
a tiny figure – it seems
as if he had gone to sleep,
like the owl in the fork of the tree.

Here, at my place,
no one is fishing, no heron
will screech, the blueish castle
ceases to be a castle, the fight
in my room will cast no folds.

A pinch of powder dissolved in oil,
that is all, and spread on a board.
What I see is absent,
a *trompe-l'œil*. I ask
for deception,
I wish to deceive.
Art's supposed to be sacred,
Heaven knows why.
Beneath the bridge I see foaming
white lead, malachite, verdigris,
fresher than water.

Der Augenschein

Du sagst:
Ich mache die Augen auf und sehe was da ist
zum Beispiel dort an der Wand diese nackte Frau da
oder hier diesen öden Bleistift
oder das Auge das mich unaufhörlich anstarrt zum Verrücktwerden
Ich mache die Augen zu und sehe was nicht da ist

So einfach ist das
So leicht bist du zu täuschen

Denn in Wirklichkeit steht die Wirklichkeit Kopf
auch dein Kopf auch das Kino in deinem Kopf

Woher weißt du ob sich das Auge bewegt und das Bild steht still
oder das Auge steht still und das Bild bewegt sich?

Sicher ist nur daß das Verschwundene nicht verschwunden ist
und das Vorhandene nicht vorhanden

Entweder du siehst das Kino oder den Film
entweder das Auge oder das Bild

Und deshalb starrst du unaufhörlich diese nackte Frau an
die sich nicht bewegt
mit aufgerissenen Augen zum Verrücktwerden
diese Frau die nicht da ist
und blickst mit geschlossenen Augen auf diese öde Brille hier
auf dieses Massaker im Kino
auf diese Gegenstände die vor dir auf dem Tisch tanzen

So einfach ist das
So leicht bist du zu täuschen

Oder du blickst in ein paar Augen in denen sich deine Augen spiegeln
in denen sich ein Paar Augen spiegeln in die du blickst

Appearances

You say:
I open my eyes and see what is there
for instance there on the wall this female nude
or this dreary pencil down here
or the eye that stares at me so incessantly, it could drive me mad
I close my eyes and see what is not there.

It's as simple as that
That easily you're deceived

For in reality reality stands on its head
and so does your head and the cinema in your head

How can you know whether the eye moves and the image stays fixed
Or the eye stays fixed and the image moves?

All that's sure is that the vanished thing has not vanished
and the present thing is not present

Either you see the cinema or the film
either the eye or the image

And that's why you stare incessantly at this female nude
who does not move
with eyes so wide-open, it could drive you mad
this woman who isn't there
and with your eyes closed look at this dreary pair of glasses
at this massacre on the screen
at these objects dancing in front of you on the table

It's as simple as that
That easily you're deceived

Or you look into a pair of eyes that mirror your eyes
that mirror a pair of eyes into which you look

Mach die Augen auf und das Erscheinende ist verschwunden
Mach die Augen zu und das Verschwundene erscheint

Aber das siehst du nicht ein
Du sagst:
Ich mache die Augen auf und sehe was da ist

usw. ad infinitum

Open your eyes and the thing that appeared has vanished
Close your eyes and the thing that vanished appears

But you won't see that
You say:
I open my eyes and see what is there

etc. ad infinitum

Das leere Blatt

Das, was du jetzt in der Hand hältst, ist beinah weiß,
aber nicht ganz; etwas ganz Weißes gibt es nicht;
es ist glatt, hart, zäh, dünn, und für gewöhnlich
knistert es, fließt, knirscht, reißt, beinah geruchlos;
und so wie es ist, bleibt es nicht; es bedeckt sich
mit Lügen, saugt alle Schrecken auf, alle Widersprüche,
Träume, Ängste, Künste, Tränen, Begierden;
bis sie getrocknet sind, vergilbt, stockig, grau;
bis es aufweicht, im Regen, zerfällt, im Müll,
immer weniger wird; nur das beste vielleicht
– an dem vielleicht das, was keiner geschrieben hat,
das Beste ist: ein Fisch, ein Salzfaß, ein Stern,
ein Einhorn, ein Elefant oder ein Ochsenkopf,
Zeichen des Heiligen Lukas; das, was erscheint,
wenn du es gegen das Licht hältst – hält,
vielleicht, tausend Jahre, oder noch eine Minute.

The Blank Sheet

What you're holding now in your hand is almost white,
but not quite; there is no such thing as a pure white thing;
it is smooth, hard, tough, thin and usually
it rustles, flows, crackles, tears, almost odourless;
and does not remain what it is; it covers itself
with lies, absorbs all the horrors, contradictions,
dreams, anxieties, skills, tears, desires;
until they desiccate, yellowing, spotted, grey;
until it grows sodden, in rain, disintegrates, as rubbish,
becomes less and less; only the best perhaps –
of which that, perhaps, which no one has written
is best of all: a fish, a salt cellar, star,
a unicorn, an elephant or an ox head,
the emblem of St Luke; that which appears
when you hold it against the light – lasts
a thousand years, perhaps, or another minute.

Konsistenz

Der Gedanke
hinter den Gedanken.
Ein Kiesel, gewöhnlich,
unvermischt, hart,
nicht zu verkaufen.

Löst sich nicht auf,
steht nicht
zur Diskussion,
ist was er ist,
nimmt nicht zu oder ab.

Unregelmäßig,
nicht bunt, geädert.
Nicht neu, nicht alt.
Braucht keine Begründung,
verlangt keinen Glauben.

Du weißt nicht, woher
du ihn hast, wohin
er geht, wozu
er dient. Ohne ihn
wärst du wenig.

Consistency

The thought
behind the thought.
A pebble, ordinary,
homogeneous, hard,
not for sale.

Does not dissolve,
is not
debatable,
is what it is,
does not gain or lose weight.

Irregular,
not brightly coloured, not veined.
Not new, not old.
Needs no substantiation,
demands no belief.

You don't know where
you get it from, where
it's going, what purpose
it serves. Without it
you wouldn't be much.

Alte Revolution

Ein Käfer, der auf dem Rücken liegt.
Die alten Blutflecken sind noch da, im Museum.
Jahrzehnte, die sich totstellen.
Ein saurer Mundgeruch dringt aus dreißig Ministerien.
Im Hotel Nacional spielen vier verstorbene Musikanten
den Tango von 1959, Abend für Abend:
Quizás, quizás, quizás.

Im Gemurmel der tropischen Maiandacht
fallen der Geschichte die Augen zu.
Nur die Sehnsucht nach Zahnpasta,
Glühbirnen und Spaghetti
liegt schlaflos da zwischen feuchten Laken.

Ein Somnambule vor zehn Mikrophonen,
der kein Ende findet, schärft seiner müden Insel ein:
Nach mir kommt nichts mehr.
Es ist erreicht.
An den Maschinenpistolen glänzt das Öl.
Der Zucker klebt in den Hemden.
Die Prostata tut es nicht mehr.

Sehnsüchtig sucht der greise Krieger
den Horizont ab nach einem Angreifer.
Aber die Kimm ist leer. Auch der Feind
hat ihn vergessen.

Old Revolution

A beetle lying on its back.
The old bloodspots are still on show
in the museum. Decades playing dead.
A sour smell from the mouth of thirty ministries.
At the Hotel Nacional four deceased musicians
are playing night by night the tango from '59:
Quizás, quizás, quizás.

By the murmur of a tropical rosary
History is taking a nap. Only those
who long for toothpaste, light bulbs
and spaghetti are tossing sleeplessly
between the damp bedsheets.

A sleepwalker in front of ten microphones
is preaching to his tired island:
After me nothing will follow.
It is finished.
The machine-guns glisten with oil.
The shirts are sticky with cane-juice.
The prostate has had it.

Wistfully the aged warrior
scans the horizon for an aggressor.
There is no one in sight. Even the enemy
has forgotten about him.

Restlicht

Doch doch, ich gehöre auch zu denen,
die es hier aushalten. Leicht sogar,
im Vergleich zu Kattowitz oder Montevideo.
Hie und da Reste von Landschaft,
rostende Eisenbahnschienen, Hummeln.
Ein kleiner Fluß, Erlen und Haselnüsse,
weil das Geld nicht gereicht hat
zur Begradigung. Über dem trüben Wasser
das Summen der Hochspannungsmasten
stört mich nicht. Es redet mir ein,
daß ich noch eine Weile lang
lesen könnte, bevor es dunkel wird.
Und wenn ich mich langweilen will,
ist das Fernsehen da, der farbige Wattebausch
auf den Augen, während draußen
die kindlichen Selbstmörder auf ihren Hondas
um den nassen Platz heulen. Auch der Krach,
auch die Rachsucht ist noch ein Lebenszeichen.
Im halben Licht vor dem Einschlafen
keine Kolik, kein wahrer Schmerz.
Wie einen leichten Muskelkater
spüren wir gähnend, sie und ich,
die von Minute zu Minute
kleiner werdende Zeit.

Residual Light

Oh yes, I, too, am one of those
who can stand it here. Easily, I would say,
compared to Katowice or Montevideo.
There are bits of landscape left
if you look for them, rusty rails,
humble-bees, alder and hazelnut on the bank
of a river spared by the engineers
for lack of development funds. I do not mind
the hum of the high-tension wires
above the murky waters. They would have me believe
that I could read for a while
before the lights go out.
And if I want to be bored,
there is the TV's colourful cotton wad
for the eyes, while outside
infantile suicides are circling the wet square
on their howling Hondas. Even the noise,
the resentment are signs of life.
In the half-light before I go to sleep
I feel no colic, no real pain.

Verschwundene Arbeit

Ziemlich entlegen, das alles.
Dunkel wie eine Sage.
Der Lumpenhändler
mit dem zerbeulten Zylinder,
des Waidmüllers blaue Hand,
der Pfragner in seinem kühlen Gewölb.

Der Schlözer stieg aus dem Schilf,
es ließ der Zedler die Beute stehn,
der Köhler den Quandel.
Die Kremplerin warf die Distel hin,
der Mollenhauer den Beitel.
Vermoderte Werke,
ausgestorbene Fertigkeiten.

Wo ist der Blatthaken geblieben,
die Zugöse, der Kammdeckel?
Verschollen der Schirrmacher,
nur der Name steht noch,
wie in Bernstein erstarrt,
im Telefonbuch.

Aber den schimmernden Quader aus Licht
habe ich selbst noch gesehen,
mit eigenen Augen, zauberhaft
mühelos in die Höhe geworfen
am eisernen Haken
auf das lederne Schulterblatt

des Eismanns, am Mittwoch,
pünktlich, die Splitter
schmolzen mir feurig
im kalten Mund.

Vanished Work

Rather remote, all of it.
As in a saga, darkly,
the rag-and-bone-man
with his battered top hat,
the blue hand of the woad-miller,
the corn-chandler in his cool cellar.

The rush-man has deserted his reed,
the beekeeper his hive,
the charcoal burner his flue.
The woolcarder threw her teasel away,
the trough-maker his chisel.
Trades mouldered away,
extinct skills.

What has happened to the bridoons,
the hames and the terrets?
The cartwright has passed away.
Only his name survives,
like an insect congealed in amber,
in the telephone book.

But the shimmering block of light
I have lived to see
with my own eyes, heaved
easily, as if by magic
with an iron hook
onto the leathery shoulder-strap

of the iceman, on Wednesdays
at noon, punctually, and the chips
melted like fire
in my chill mouth.

Der Eisenwarenladen

Zwei ältliche Waisen,
die ihn geerbt haben,
neunzehnjährig,
vor neunzehn Jahren.

Nonnen in verwaschenen Schürzen,
eingemauert
von bleiernen Schubladen,
Stifte und Stellschrauben
zwischen den Lippen.

Ihr grauer Eifer,
ihre rosige Hingabe
unter der nackten Glühbirne.
Der graue Geruch nach Schmierfett,
Gummi, Kitt und Metall.

Riesige Rohrzangen, Herzbohrer
in ungeliebten Händen.
Die feuchte Zunge,
die sich nach dem Mundwinkel sehnt
beim Schreiben der Rechnung.

Ursuppe, hast du dir davon
etwas träumen lassen?
Was hast du dir, Weltgeist,
dabei gedacht?
Vorsehung, war das alles:

Zwei ältliche Schwestern,
lebenslänglich,
in einem Eisenwarenladen?
Ihr rosiger Eifer,
ihre graue Hingabe
an das Schmirgelpapier?

The Ironmonger's Shop

Two elderly orphans
who inherited it
when they were nineteen,
nineteen years ago.

Nuns in washed-out aprons,
walled in by leaden chests
of drawers,
tacks and adjusting screws
between their lips.

Their rosy devotion,
their greying eagerness
under the naked light bulb,
the grey smell of grease,
of rubber, metal and putty.

Enormous wrenches, breast drills
in unloved hands.
The moist tongue
longing for another mouth
while the bill is made out.

Is this what you dreamt of,
Primal Soup? *Weltgeist*,
did you have your wits about you?
Was that all you had in mind,
Divine Providence?

Two elderly sisters
imprisoned for life
in an ironmonger's shop?
Their rosy eagerness,
their grey devotion
to the emery-paper?

Alte Ehepaare

Wer so lange geblieben ist,
macht sich wenig vor.

»Ich weiß, daß ich nichts weiß«:
Auch das ist noch übertrieben.

Alte Ehepaare
haben nichts übrig
für das Überflüssige,
lassen das Unentscheidbare
in der Schwebe.

Merkwürdig distanziert,
dieser luzide Blick.
Kühne Rückzüge,
geplant
von langer Hand.

Andrerseits hartnäckig
wie der Schachtelhalm.
Resignation –
ein Fremdwort.

Improvisierte Krücken,
Selbsthilfe, Kartoffeln
im eigenen Garten
und im Zweifelsfall,
am Kreuzweg,
die Sauerstoffmaske zur Hand.

Man sieht manches,
wenn das Licht ausgeht.

Old Couples

Those who have stayed so long
don't kid themselves much.

'I know that I know nothing':
even that would be an exaggeration.

Old married couples
have no use for overstatements;
they leave open
what cannot be settled.

Their glance is lucid
and strangely distant.
Bold retreats,
planned
long in advance.

On the other hand
they are dogged like marestail.
Resignation
is Greek to them.

Improvised crutches,
self-help, homegrown potatoes,
and if the worst,
comes to the worst,
at the crossroads,
the oxygen mask at hand.

There is much to be seen
when the lights go out.

Valse triste et sentimentale

Ja, früher, früher!
Und was ist jetzt?
Mach was du willst,
aber sei so lieb:
Keine Rechtfertigungen.

Mit oder ohne,
du hast jedenfalls.
Beziehungsweise
du hast nicht.
Das genügt.

»Was soll ich *denn* machen?
Was soll ich *denn* machen?«
Natürlich. Das kennt man.
Das fragen sie immer,
wenn es zu spät ist.

Eigentlich schade.
Manchmal vermiß ich dich schon
mit deinen ewigen Dramen,
deinen blöden Ausreden,
deinem faulen Zauber.

Ich, schlechtes Gewissen?
Da kann ich nur lachen.
Mach die Tür zu
und laß dich nie wieder
blicken!

Valse triste et sentimentale

Blast the old days.
What about now?
Do as you like,
but please,
no apologies.

You did, didn't you?
With or without it.
Or else
you didn't.
That's all there is to it.

'What do you want me to do?
What do you want me to do?'
Of course. I know.
That's what they all ask
when it's too late.

A pity, really.
Sometimes I begin to miss you
with your eternal scenes,
your foggy excuses,
your hocus pocus.

Me, feeling guilty?
You make me laugh.
Get out of here
and don't show your face again,
ever.

Fetisch

Immer nur
an diesen Flaum
denkt er nachts
kleiner
als eine Hand
und weiter
denkt er
an nichts
Nichts anderes
ist da
als dieses Büschel
das nicht da ist
Er stellt es sich
dunkel vor
dieses Gewölle
wie es sich bauscht
hell
Er hört förmlich
wie es knistert
unter dem Druck
der Hand
Er sieht
wie es sich kräuselt
im Licht
blond schwarz
wie es glitzert
wahnsinnig
weich und widerspenstig
und nicht weiter
nennenswert

Fetish

All night
he is thinking of it
a wisp of down
smaller
than the hand of a man
There is nothing else
he can think of
there is nothing
but this tuft of hair
which is not here
He imagines it
dark
a woolly mass
curling
brightly
He can almost hear it
rustle
at the touch of his hand
He sees it
bristling
in the light
blonde black
soft and unruly
glittering madly
and scarcely worth
further notice

Schlaftablette

Bunte Raumkapsel
winziges Senfkorn der Amnesie
das seinen Kern entblößt
in der Neige der Sintflut

Weißer Taifun im Wasserglas
chemischer Katarakt
den ich austrinke
der mich ertränkt

Schlieriges *chiaroscuro*
Blauer Nil
der mein Gehirn marmoriert
bis ich untergetaucht bin

Stilles Mirakel
aus zentnerschweren Milligrammen
in dem ich meine Angst aus-
hauche und meine Freude

bis tief in den schrillen Tag

Sleeping Pill

Gaudy space capsule
tiny mustard seed of amnesia
revealing its core
in the lees of the deluge

White typhoon in a glass of water
chemical cataract
which I drain
in which I drown

Cloudy *chiaroscuro*
Blue Nile
marbling my brain
until I am submerged

Mute miracle bearing down
grain by grain like a hundredweight
You help me to breathe my last worry
and my last joy

until the next shrill noon

Zum Ewigen Frieden

Dieses Zeug, das aus dem dunklen
Himmel hell fällt, leicht,
gleichmäßig, lautlos, ohne
Aufenthalt tänzelnd, setzt sich

auf alles, ohne Eile, was eckig
ist, Hochhaus, Briefkasten, Sarg.
Alles, was eckig war, wird
rund, langsam bauschen sich

Mauern, der Abdruck der Schuhe
füllt sich, geht unter, mild,
es versinkt die Schaufel,
langsam, langsam, alles, was

zählbar war, spitz, distinkt,
fließt ineinander, Dachziegel,
Köpfe, behaubt sich, es unterliegt
das Schroffe dem Weichen, es weicht

der Unterschied, niedrig, hoch,
flach, erhaben, böse, gut. Da
der Hügel war vor Wochen, Tagen,
Minuten ein Puff, eine Bretterbude,

ein Schneepflug. Auch die Zeit
ist zu Watte geworden. Hie und da
noch ein Wetterhahn, eine Antenne.
Die leichte Wölbung am Horizont

undeutlich, von Flocken verschluckt,
muß das Matterhorn sein, oder
der Ararat. Es verschwindet der Krieg
im Frieden, weiß und vollkommen.

Towards Eternal Peace

All this light stuff falling down
from the dark sky brightly,
prancing without respite,
without a sound, evenly

squatting, without haste,
on all things square,
building coffin letterbox.
All things square bulge

slowly, walls billow, footprints
fill up and are erased,
mildly, the shovel sinks
into oblivion, slowly, slowly,

all things countable,
sharp, distinct, merge
and become submerged, heads
and roofs are hooded, rigour

gives way to softness, differences
dwindle: low, high, uneven, flat,
good, evil. Weeks, days, minutes ago
the hill over there was a booth,

a brothel, a snow-plow. Time, too,
has turned into cotton wool.
Goodbye to the weather-cock, the antenna.
That slight bulge in the horizon,

embalmed by flakes, shrouded
in vagueness, must be the Matterhorn,
or Mount Ararat. War dissolves
into peace, white and perfect.

Alles gleichmäßig wie der Schnee,
nur der Schnee nicht. Jeder Kristall
für sich, verschieden von
jedem Kristall. Ein Blick

durch das Mikroskop genügt, nur
schade, daß es versunken ist,
das Mikroskop, und das Auge
verdunkelt vom Schnee.

All things even out in the snow,
except the snow. Each crystal
is on its own, differing
from the next, as a glance

through the microscope would show.
A pity that it has gone under,
our microscope, and the eye
is blacked out by the snow.

Ein Hase im Rechenzentrum

Die schnellste Maschine,
Parallelarchitektur,
knapp tausend Megaflops,
vermag seinem kleinen Gehirn
nicht zu folgen.

Die bebende Oberlippe
zuckend im Neonlicht,
die großen Augen starr
auf den Bildschirm gerichtet,
trommelt er panisch
gegen das graue Linoleum.

Dann, es ist drei Uhr früh,
der letzte Plasmaphysiker
ist nach Hause gegangen,
schnellt er plötzlich hoch
und jagt im Zickzack
zwischen Monitoren
und stotternden Druckern
durch den verlassenen Raum.

Weicher Feigling,
fünfzig Millionen Jahre
älter als wir!
Dem Blutdurst der Jäger,
der Ramme, dem Gas,
dem Virus entkommen,
schlägt er ungerührt seine Haken.

Aus dem Eozän hoppelt er
an uns vorbei in eine Zukunft,
reich an Feinden,
doch nahrhaft und geil
wie der Löwenzahn.

A Hare in the Data Processing Centre

The fastest of our machines,
parallel architecture,
close to a thousand megaflops,
cannot keep up
with its miniscule brain.

Its upper lip in a quiver
it twitches in the neon glare,
the large eyes staring fixedly
at the monitor screen,
it panics, its hindleg drumming
against the grey lino floor.

Past three o'clock in the morning,
when the last plasma physicist
has gone home, it suddenly jumps
and zigzags in a wild chase
past work stations
and stuttering printers
through the deserted hall.

Soft coward,
fifty million years
older than we are!
Having survived
rammer, poison gas, virus,
it goes on intrepidly
doubling the hunters.

Out of the eocene
it hobbles past us into a future
rich in enemies
but nourishing and rank
like dandelion.

Limbisches System

Es ist alt, es ist weich,
es versteht sich nicht,
weiß nicht, was *limbus* bedeutet,
was ein System ist.

Zwischen Gewölbe und Balken
eine Vorhölle, winzig.

Ammonshorn, Gürtel, Mandelkern:
ein dunkles Gedächtnis,
das sich seiner selbst
nicht erinnern kann.

Unkontrollierbar
kontrolliert es
Angst Lust Mord Sucht

Seine Schleifen und Fasern
ein Kabelbaum
tief im Schädel,
intra- und extramural.

Kriechströme, Schwelbrände,
Kurzschlüsse.
Kleine Defekte,
die rasch eskalieren.

Ein Ruck in der Steuerung,
und es nimmt Rache.
Ein elektrischer Stoß,
und es läuft Amok.

Ein paar Milliarden Zellen
im Dunkeln. Das Menschengeschlecht,
ein winziges Knäuel
zwischen Anfang und Amnesie.

Limbic System

It is ancient, it is spongy,
does not understand itself,
has no idea what *limbus* means,
what a system is.

Between fornix and corpus callosum
a minuscule limbo.

Ammon's horn, belt, amygdala:
a dark memory
unable to recall itself.

It controls
fear lust murder addiction,
and no one controls it.

Its loops and fibres
pass through a cable duct
intra- and extra-murally
hidden in the depth of the skull.

Prone to leakage currents,
cable burnouts, short circuits.
Small faults
which escalate quickly.

An excessive input
and hell will break loose.
An electric shock
and it will run amuck.

A few billion cells in the dark.
Man manhandled
by a lump in the brain
between birth and amnesia.

Das Gift

Nicht, wie es früher war, rund,
wenig, ein Gran, verschlossen
wie eine Beere, wie eine Erbse
klein, verborgen in einem Ring,
einer Kapsel, privat, minimal,
heimlich wie eine fixe Idee,

sondern offenbar wie ein Meer,
schwerwiegend und normal,
breit verteilt, wie der Wind
entfesselt, wolkig, geruchlos
und ebensowenig zu fassen, all-
gegenwärtig wie früher Gott,

der, ein privates Gran,
wenig, immer weniger wiegt,
wie eine Erbse, heimlich,
wie eine Tollkirsche
in der Brust, verschlossen
wie eine fixe Idee.

The Poison

Not, as it used to be, round,
little, a grain, sealed
like a berry, a pea,
tiny, concealed in a ring,
a capsule, private, minimal,
secret like an *idée fixe*,

but manifest like the sea,
ponderous and normal,
widely distributed, like the wind
unleashed, cloudy, odourless
and as impalpable, omni-
present as God was once

who, a private grain,
little, weighs less and less,
like a pea, secret,
like a deadly nightshade seed
in one's breast, sealed
like an *idée fixe*.

Vorgänger

Abgewandt, früher
oder später, abgewandt
haben sie sich,
einer nach dem andern.
Zuerst die Augen,
unmerklich, dann
diese minimale Geste
der linken Hand,
die zu deuten
uns nicht gegeben war.

Ein Abwinken,
ein ironischer Gruß:
»Wir stellen anheim,
lassen auf sich beruhn.«
Aber was?

Erst, als wir
das glatte Kissen fanden,
die leere Tasse,
das Hemd über dem Stuhl,
den Schlüssel am Brett,
waren wir irritiert.

»Was hast du?«
Keine Antwort.
Weder Vorwurf
noch Nachsicht.
Nicht einmal das Licht
haben sie ausgemacht
im Korridor.

Dann sind sie
kleiner geworden,
immer kleiner,
wie Flugzeuge, oder

Precursors

Turned away, sooner
or later, they have
turned away,
one after the other.
First the eyes,
imperceptibly, then
this minimal gesture
of the left hand
which to construe
was beyond our gift.

A waving aside,
an ironic greeting:
'We leave it open,
we let the matter rest.'
But what?

Only when we
found the smooth cushion,
the empty cup,
the shirt across the chair,
the key hung up,
we were annoyed.

'What's biting you?'
No answer.
Neither reproach
nor consideration.
They didn't even
switch off the light
in the corridor.

Then they grew smaller,
smaller and smaller
like aircraft, or
when they walked,

wenn sie zu Fuß waren,
im Schnee, dunkel,
auf Knüppeldämmen,
in einer Staubwolke.

Was aus ihnen geworden ist,
wissen wir nicht.

in snow, dark,
on log roads,
in a cloud of dust.

What's become of them
we do not know.

Abtrift

Das Gehirn im Sinkflug,
immer tiefer.
An den Spanndrähten
zerrt der Abwind.
Das Steuer flattert,
schlägt aus,
»von selbst«.
Auch eine Musik:
rauschende Luft,
knirschendes Holz.
Es knackt im Holm,
im Ohr, im Kopf.
Schmerzloser Sog,
selbstvergessen,
feierlich leichtes
Gleiten, dem
Dunkleren zu.

Leeway

The brain on its descent,
lower and lower.
Against the tension wires
the down-draught tugs.
The rudder flutters,
veers
'by itself'.
A music too:
rushing air,
creaking timbers.
There's a crack in the spar,
in the ear, in the head.
Painless suction,
self-oblivious,
solemnly weightless
gliding towards
the darker place.

Seltsamer Attraktor

Minuten-, stunden-, tagelang
gebeugt über das Geländer.
über Millionen
von unlösbaren Gleichungen,
seh ich ins Aug des Zyklons,
der mir ins Auge sieht;

kalkgrün, weißschäumend
rauscht die helle Materie,
hypnotisch kreisend,
die glitzernde Gischt,
in wiederkehrenden Strudeln
nie wiederkehrend;

und obenauf, flaumig,
im Schaum, im Licht,
taumelt, tanzt etwas Nasses,
Braunes, das tanzt,
aber nicht untergeht,
taumelt ein Teddybär.

Strange Attractor

Bent over the railing
for minutes hours days,
over millions of equations
with no solution in sight,
I look into the eye of a cyclone
that looks me straight in the eye;

chalky green, foamy white
live matter roaring on
in hypnotic swirls,
turning in bright eddies
and glittering cycles
which never recur;

and on top of the foam,
wet, brown and downy,
bobbing up and down,
rolling dizzily in the light
but not going under,
tumbles a teddy bear.

KIOSK

KIOSK

(1995)

Privilegierte Tatbestände

Es ist verboten, Personen in Brand zu stecken.

Es ist verboten, Personen in Brand zu stecken, die im Besitz einer gültigen Aufenthaltsgenehmigung sind.

Es ist verboten, Personen in Brand zu stecken, die sich an die gesetzlichen Bestimmungen halten und im Besitz einer gültigen Aufenthaltsgenehmigung sind.

Es ist verboten, Personen in Brand zu stecken, von denen nicht zu erwarten ist, daß sie den Bestand und die Sicherheit der Bundesrepublik Deutschland gefährden.

Es ist verboten, Personen in Brand zu stecken, soweit sie nicht durch ihr Verhalten dazu Anlaß geben.

Es ist insbesondere auch Jugendlichen, die angesichts mangelnder Freizeitangebote und in Unkenntnis der einschlägigen Bestimmungen sowie aufgrund von Orientierungsschwierigkeiten psychisch gefährdet sind, nicht gestattet, Personen ohne Ansehen der Person in Brand zu stecken.

Es ist mit Rücksicht auf das Ansehen der Bundesrepublik Deutschland im Ausland dringend davon abzuraten.

Es gehört sich nicht.

Es ist nicht üblich.

Es sollte nicht zur Regel werden.

Es muß nicht sein.

Niemand ist dazu verpflichtet.

Es darf niemandem zum Vorwurf gemacht werden, wenn er es unterläßt, Personen in Brand zu stecken.

Jedermann genießt ein Grundrecht auf Verweigerung.

Entsprechende Anträge sind an das zuständige Ordnungsamt zu richten.

Nota bene. Wer diesen Text in eine andere Sprache überträgt, wird gebeten, an Stelle der Bundesrepublik Deutschland versuchsweise die offizielle Bezeichnung seines eigenen Landes einzusetzen. Diese Fußnote sollte auch in der Übersetzung stehenbleiben.

Privileged Instructions

It is forbidden to set fire to persons.

It is forbidden to set fire to persons in possession of a valid residence permit.

It is forbidden to set fire to persons who comply with Government regulations and are in possession of a valid residence permit.

It is forbidden to set fire to persons not suspected of endangering the constitution and security of the German Federal Republic.

It is forbidden to set fire to persons whose behaviour and attitudes are not conducive to that suspicion.

More specifically, juveniles, too, who in view of deficient leisure facilities and in ignorance of the relevant regulations or because of difficulties of orientation are psychically endangered, are not permitted to set fire to persons indiscriminately.

Indeed that course is urgently inadvisable in consideration of the German Federal Republic's reputation abroad.

It is not seemly.

It is not usual.

It is not to become the rule.

It is not necessary.

No one is obliged to do it.

No one is to be blamed if he or she refrains from setting fire to persons.

It is everyone's basic right to refuse to do so.

Relevant applications should be submitted to the regulatory office responsible.

NB. Anyone translating this text into another language is requested to try substituting the official designation of his or her country for the German Federal Republic. This footnote is to be retained in a translation.

Translator's note: This would call for a translation much more free than the one provided. It is the reader who is invited to try out that substitution in his or her mind, with appropriate modifications of terminology and reference.

Die Reichen

Wo sie nur immer wieder herkommen,
diese üppigen Horden! Nach jedem Debakel
sind sie aus den Ruinen gekrochen,
ungerührt; durch jedes Nadelöhr
sind sie geschlüpft,
zahl-, stein- und segensreich.

Die Ärmsten. Niemand mag sie.
Schwer tragen sie an ihrer Last.
Sie beleidigen uns,
sind an allem schuld,
können nichts dafür,
müssen weg.

Wir haben alles versucht.
Gepredigt haben wir ihnen,
beschworen haben wir sie,
und erst als es nicht anders ging,
erpreßt, enteignet, geplündert.
Wir haben sie bluten lassen
und an die Wand gestellt.

Aber kaum ließen wir die Flinte sinken
und nahmen in ihren Sesseln Platz,
stellten wir fest, ungläubig
zuerst, dann aber aufatmend:
auch gegen uns war kein Kraut gewachsen.
Dochdoch, man gewöhnt sich an alles.
Bis zum nächsten Mal.

The Rich

Wherever do they keep on coming from,
these luxurious hordes! After every collapse
they've crept out of the ruins,
unmoved; through every eye of a needle
they've slipped,
rich in number, good heels and blessings.

Those wretches. Nobody likes them.
Their burden bows them down.
They offend us,
are to blame for everything,
can't help it,
must be got rid of.

We've tried everything.
We've preached to them,
we've implored them,
and only when there was no other way
blackmailed, expropriated, plundered them.
We have left them to bleed
and put them against the wall.

But no sooner did we lower the rifle
and seated ourselves in their armchairs
than we knew, incredulous
at first, but then with a sigh of relief:
we too were irrepressible.
Yes, yes, one gets used to anything.
Till it happens again.

Der blecherne Teller

Über die Armut ist alles gesagt.
Daß sie hartnäckig ist, zäh, klebrig.
Daß sie niemanden interessiert,
außer die Armen. Langweilig ist sie.
So emsig, daß ihr keine Zeit bleibt,
über Langeweile zu klagen.
Sie ist wie der Dreck. Dort,
wo unten ist, ist sie,
stört, steckt an, stinkt.

Sie fällt auf durch Allgegenwart.
Es ist, als wäre sie ewig.
Göttliche Attribute. Hilfreiche,
Heilige suchen sie, Mönche
und Nonnen sind mit ihr verlobt.
Alle andern, lebenslänglich
auf der Flucht vor ihr, holt sie
mit ihrem blechernen Teller
majestätisch und unbewegt

an der nächsten Ecke ein.

The Tin Plate

About poverty all has been said:
that it's tenacious, sticky, persistent
and of no interest to anybody
save the poor. It is boring.
It has too much to worry about
to complain about boredom.
Like dirt, it is to be found
way down. It's contagious,
smelly, a nuisance.

Its omnipresence is striking.
It seems to partake of eternity.
Attributes which are divine.
Helpers and saints seek it.
Monks and nuns are betrothed to it.
With the rest of us,
all our lives on the run,
poverty catches up
at the next street-corner,

unmoving, unmoved, majestic,
tin-plate in hand.

Eine Beobachtung beim Austausch von Funktionseliten

Dieses schürfende Geräusch,
ein Scharren, Tag und Nacht,
von Zehen, Fingern, Krallen –
das kommt vom Kratzen,
vom Klettern, vom Krabbeln derer,
die da mit angehaltenem Atem
hochwollen, hoch,

immer höher, voll Angst,
Angst, daß der sandige Hang
nachgibt unter den Nägeln,
so, daß sie abwärts, dahin,
wo sie herkamen, rutschen,
und zwar, je mehr sie, in Panik,
noch ehe die mürbe Kante

bröselt, bricht, auf allem,
was sie unter sich vermuten,
anfangen herumzutrampeln,
desto tiefer, unaufhaltsam,

nach unten

An Observation on Shifts in Functional Elites

This abrasive noise,
a scraping by day and night,
of toes, fingers, claws –
this comes of the scratching,
the climbing, the crawling of those
who with their breath held
want to rise, high,

higher and higher, full of fear,
the fear that the sandy slope
will give way under their nails
so that down, to the place
they came from, they will slide
and the more, in their panic,
even before the brittle edge

crumbles, breaks, on all
they suppose to be below them
they start to trample,
the more, ineluctably,

downward

Altes Europa

Im warmen Brotduft vor der Bäckerei
hält ein dicker Zauberer aus Guinea
unter der goldenen Brezel
Schlüsselanhänger feil
in der Graubrüdergasse.
(Wer waren die Grauen Brüder?)

Kleine drahtige Dealer
in riesigen Turnschuhen streiten sich
in einer Sprache knurrend,
die niemand versteht, an der Mauer
des Kirchhofs zum Heiligen Geist.
(Wer war der Heilige Geist?)

Und dann die alte Bosnierin,
die ihr steifes Bein ausstreckt,
ein paar Minuten lang, auf einer Bank
im dunkelgrünen, stillen Hof
hinter dem dunkelgrünen Portal
des Hauses zum Elefanten, erbaut 1639.

Old Europe

In the warm bread smell in front of the bakery
a fat magician from Guinea
under the golden pretzel offers
key-ring pendants for sale
in Graubrüdergasse.
(Who were those Greyfriars?)

Little wiry dealers
in huge trainers growling
quarrel in a language
nobody understands, by the wall
of the Holy Ghost churchyard.
(Who was the Holy Ghost?)

And then the old Bosnian woman
stretching her stiff legs
for a few minutes on a bench
in the dark-green silent courtyard
behind the dark-green portal
of the Elephant Inn, built in 1639.

Hymne an die Dummheit

Himmelsmacht, die sich verbirgt in den Falten des Stammhirns,
bodenlose Mitgift an das Menschengeschlecht in *saecula saeculorum*,

unzählig wie die Milchstraße bist du
und vielfältig wie das Gras.

Mächtige Zwillingsschwester der Intelligenz, Händchen haltend
zelebrierst du mit ihr ein trübsinniges Palaver.

Ja, es ist stark, wie du uns inspirierst in immer neuen Verwandlungen,
als weibliche Dämlichkeit und als männliche Idiotie,

wie du aus den blutunterlaufenen Augen des Schlägers leuchtest
und einhertrippelst im aristokratisch hüstelnden Dünkel,

wie du uns anwehst mit dem Mundgeruch einer beschickerten Muse
und als vielsilbiges Delirieren im philosophischen Seminar.

Was wäre der Tüchtige ohne dich, stock-, stroh- und hundsdumme
    Dummheit,
die feurig durch seine Adern rollt wie eine Überdosis Amphetamin,

und der Forscher ohne die fixe Idee, der er durch die weißen Korridore
seines Instituts hinterherrappelt wie die Ratte im Labyrinth!

Gar nicht zu gedenken der Weltgeschichte, wessen gedächte sie denn,
wenn nicht der Sieger in ihrem napoleonischen Stumpfsinn.

So wird uns wohl der dümmliche Stolz des Gewinners erhalten bleiben
und der dumpfe Groll des Verlierers, nur hie und da versüßt

durch den erleuchteten Sums der Sektenprediger,
der Komiker und Quartalssäufer. Dummheit,

oft Verleumdete, die du dich in deiner Schlauheit
dümmer stellst als du bist, Beschützerin aller Hinfälligen,

Ode to Stupidity

Heavenly power that hides in the folds of the tribal brain,
bottomless dowry to the human race *in saecula saeculorum*,

numberless as the Milky Way you are
and multiple as grass.

Mighty twin sister of intelligence, holding hands
together with her you celebrate the dim-witted palaver.

Yes, it's impressive, how you inspire us in transformations
ever new, as feminine daftness and masculine idiocy,

how you shine from the bloodshot eyes of the hooligan
and trip along in upper-class arrogance clearing its throat,

and how you waft at us with a bedraggled Muse's bad breath
and as polysyllabic delirium in the philosophy seminar.

What would the efficient man be without you, stick-, straw-,
    goose-brained Stupidity
that, fiery, runs through his veins like an overdose of amphetamine,

and the researcher without his idée fixe he goes chasing after
down his institute's white corridors like a rat in a maze!

Not to mention the History of the World in which
only the victors are mentioned in their Napoleonic dullness.

So the winner's witless pride will be preserved for us
and the loser's vague resentment, only here and there sweetened

by the illumined fuss of the sectarian preachers,
the comedians and dipsomaniacs. Stupidity,

you the often maligned, who in your slyness
often pretend to be stupider than you are, protector of all the frail,

nur den Auserwählten läßt du zuteilwerden deine seltenste Gabe,
die gebenedeite Einfalt der Einfältigen.

Sie sind die unbeschriebenen Blätter in deinem großen Buch,
dessen Siegel du keinem von uns eröffnest.

only to the elect do you grant the rarest of your gifts,
the blessed simplicity of the simple.

They are the blank pages in your huge book
whose seal you'll not break for any of us.

Schöner Sonntag

Der alte Herr mit dem Backenbart,
mit den zerbrechlichen Knochen,
wie er da auf dem Bänkchen sitzt
vor dem Bunker,
vor seinem eigenen Bunker.

Wie er dasitzt in der Morgensonne
und strickt und murmelt.
Was hat er gesagt?
Was hat er gesagt?
Schöner Sonntag heute.
Schöner Sonntag heute.

Wie er das Strickzeug sinken läßt,
wie er wittert,
wie er lauscht,
wie er aufpaßt,
ob einer um die Ecke kommt,
ihn totzuschlagen.

Wie er weiterstrickt,
wie er vor sich hinträllert:
Niemand da.
Niemand da.
Schöner Sonntag heute.

Nice Sunday

The old whiskered gentleman,
frail of frame, look at him
sitting there on his little bench
in front of the shelter,
in front of his very own shelter.

Look at him sitting there, knitting,
muttering in the morning sun.
What did he say?
What did he say?
Nice Sunday today.
Nice Sunday today.

Now he will drop his knitting gear,
sniffing the air
he will cock his ear,
he will watch out
for someone coming up
to bash in his head.

Look, he picks up his needles again,
humming to himself:
Nobody there.
Nobody there.
Nice Sunday today.

Von oben gesehen

Schwindelfrei
wie ein alter Dachdecker,
behende, von denen,
die auf dem Boden
der Tatsachen bleiben,
nicht weiter beachtet,
zu zaubern,

freihändig,
mit geübtem Griff,
wenn alles gut geht,
hoch oben
ein unscheinbares Wunder
zu vollbringen,

ja, das ist,
aufs Ganze gesehen,
aussichtslos,
gewährt aber hie und da
schräge Blicke nach unten,
in kleinere Abgründe,
Zimmer,

wo, je nachdem,
staubsaugende Frauen
oder ächzende Freier
auf ihre Art,
doch mit rührendem Eifer
ankämpfen
gegen die Schwerkraft.

Bird's Eye View

Immune to dizziness
like an old roofer,
agile, not noticed much
by those who have their feet
on the ground of facts,
to conjure

without holding on,
with a practised grasp,
when all goes well,
high up
to bring off
an inconspicuous miracle,

yes, that,
seen all in all,
is a mug's game,
but here and there allows
slanting glances downward,
into smaller abysses,
rooms

where, as the case may be,
women with vacuum cleaners
or moaning lovers
in their way,
but with touching zeal,
contend with
the force of gravity.

Von der Algebra der Gefühle

Ich habe oft das Gefühl (brennend,
dunkel, undefinierbar usw.),
daß das Ich keine Tatsache ist,
sondern ein Gefühl,
das ich nicht loswerde.

Ich hege es, lasse ihm freien Lauf,
erwidere es, von Fall zu Fall.
Aber es ist nur eins unter vielen.

Die Menge der Gefühle ist abzählbar unendlich,
d. h. sie lassen sich im Prinzip numerieren,
bis ins Aschgraue.

Die Nummer der Eifersucht
ist offensichtlich die Sieben.
Auch die Angst ist prim.
Und ich habe das dumpfe Gefühl,
daß die Demütigung
die 188 auf ihrer Stirn trägt –
eine Zahl ohne Eigenschaften.

Auch das Gefühl, numeriert zu sein,
ist vermutlich längst numeriert,
nur wozu und von wem?

Das erhabne Gefühl des Zorns
bewohnt ein anderes Zimmer
in Hilberts Hotel
als das Gefühl,
über den Zorn erhaben zu sein.

Und nur wer sich hingeben kann
dem abstrakten Gefühl
fur die Abstraktion, der weiß,
daß es in manchen sehr hellen Nächten
den Wert $\sqrt{-1}$ anzunehmen pflegt.

On the Algebra of Feelings

I often have the feeling (intense,
obscure, indefinable etc)
that the I is not a fact
but a feeling
I can't get rid of.

I tend it, give it a free run,
reciprocate it, from case to case.
But it's only one among many.

The mass of feelings is countably infinite,
i.e. they can be numbered in principle
ad infinitum or nauseam.

The number of jealousy
evidently is seven.
Fear, too, is a prime.
And I have the vague feeling
that humiliation
bears 188 on its forehead –
a number with no qualities.

And the feeling of being numbered
presumably has long been numbered,
only what for and by whom?

The sublime feeling of anger
occupies a different room
in Hilbert's Hotel
to the feeling
of being above anger.

And only those who can apply themselves
to the abstract feeling
for abstraction know
that in some very bright nights
it will assume the value $\sqrt{-1}$.

Dann wieder läuft es mir kalt
über den Rücken, das Gefühl,
ein Paket zu sein,
das gefühllose, pelzige Gefühl,
von dem die Zunge zu bersten droht
nach der Injektion,
wenn sie dem Zahn auf den Zahn fühlt,
oder die Peinlichkeit
mit ihrem durchdringenden Bleigeschmack,
das mächtige Gefühl der Ohnmacht,
das unaufhaltsam der Null zustrebt,
und das falsche Gefühl
der wahren Empfindung
mit seinem abscheulichen Kettenbruch.

Dann erfüllt mich
eine Schnittmenge aus gemischten Gefühlen,
schuldig, fremd, wohl, verloren,
alles auf einmal.

Nur dem höchsten der Gefühle
wäre das Ich nicht gewachsen.
Statt Aufwallungen zu suchen
mit dem Limes ∞,
läßt es sich lieber
eine Minute lang übermannen
vom Schauder des eisig heißen Wassers
unter der Dusche, dessen Nummer
noch keiner entziffert hat.

Then again it sends a shiver
down my spine, the feeling
of being a parcel,
that feelingless, furry feeling
which threatens to make one's tongue burst
after the injection,
when it probes the shape of a tooth,
or embarrassment
with its pervasive taste of lead,
the powerful feeling of powerlessness
which incessantly tends towards zero,
and the false feeling
of true sensibility
with its abominable continued fraction.

Then I am filled
with a cross-section of mixed feelings,
guilty, alien, euphoric, lost,
all at the same time.

To the highest of feelings alone
the I would not be equal.
Instead of looking for upsurges
with the threshold ∞,
it would rather
be overcome for one minute
by the shudder of icily hot water
under the shower, whose number
no one has yet deciphered.

Stoßverkehr

In allen Ballungsräumen
irren Körper umher,
die zu tun haben.
Hinter der Denkerstirn
umwälzende Pläne.
Es geht um Listenplätze,
Beiwohnungsgelegenheiten,
Perückengeschäfte.

Keine Zeit, beim besten Willen,
wie Ahnen oder Geister,
die keinen Unterhalt
und keine Unterhaltung brauchen,
abgesehen von Absichten
zu schweben,

oder auch nur
sich wie diese Katze da
auf dem Teppich
zusammenzurollen,
unbedeutend anheimgegeben
dem unergründlich atmenden
ruhigen Wechsel der Stoffe.

Rush-hour Traffic

In all congested areas
bodies wander about
with something to do.
Behind the thinker's brow
revolutionising plans.
They concern election lists,
extra-marital opportunities,
wig shops.

No time, with the best will in the world,
like ancestors or ghosts
who need no upkeep
and no conversation
apart from intentions
to hover

or only to
roll themselves up
like that cat
on the carpet
unimportantly given up
to the unfathomably breathing
calm metabolic process.

Gutes Zureden

Bei jeder sich bietenden Gelegenheit
deutsch sein oder links oder maskulin
oder katholisch oder jung oder gelb,
oder intelligent, oder im Gegenteil –
nicht sehr ergiebig, mein Lieber!
Lebenslänglich herumirren als Sandwichmann
für die eigenen Eigenschaften,
das muß doch nicht sein!
Eine schwach pigmentierte Epidermis
ist schließlich kein Beruf,
und was das betrifft,
auch die Liebe zum Beruf
kann man übertreiben.

Aber ich kann doch nicht
aus meiner Haut heraus!

Zugegeben. Aber deshalb
brauchst du noch lange nicht
herumzureiten auf deiner berühmten
Identität, die weiter nichts ist
als eine tönerne Schelle
und ein Klappern im Wind.
Du könntest auch anders.
Es käme, denk es, o Seele,
auf den Versuch an.

Persuasive Talk

At every possible opportunity
to be British or Left or masculine
or Catholic or young or yellow-skinned
or intelligent, or the contrary –
not very productive, my dear!
To spend your life walking about as a sandwich man
for your own qualities,
that can't be necessary.
A poorly pigmented epidermis,
after all, is not a profession,
and, as for that,
even love for your profession
can be exaggerated.

But I can't
get out of my skin, can I?

True enough. But that's no reason
for making a fuss about
your famous identity
that is no more
than a tinkling bell
and a clattering in the wind.
You could try something different.
It's the attempt – say not
the struggle nought availeth – that matters.

Sich selbst verschluckende Sätze

Ich sage gar nichts, sagt einer,
und zappelnd auf seinem Stuhl
fährt er fort: Ich bewege mich nicht.
Ich schweige, ruft er. Ich schlafe.
Ich verspreche mich nie. Das
verspreche ich. Meine Widerlegungen
widerlege ich spielend. Ich bin,
verkündet er, der Bescheidenste,
von jeder Eitelkeit frei. Deutsch,
beteuert er, spreche ich nicht.
Von mir selber würde ich nie
und nimmer reden. Ich habe Unrecht,
wenn ich behaupte, daß ich recht habe,
wenn ich behaupte, daß ich Unrecht habe,
usw. Daß ich je ins Stottern geriete,
ist ausgeschlossen. Glaubwürdig,
wie ich bin, und bewußtlos, darf ich,
glaube ich, von mir sagen: Ich
widerspreche mir nicht. Ich
bin nicht da. Ich f-f-f-fehle.

Self-demolishing Speech Act

I'm not saying anything, he says,
and, fidgeting in his chair,
he claims: I do not move.
I keep silent, he shouts. I'm asleep.
I promise never to make a slip
of the tongue. With consummate ease
I refute all my refutations. I am,
he proclaims, the most modest of men,
devoid of vanity. He protests
that he does not speak English.
Never, he says, would I refer to myself.
I am wrong maintaining that I am right
when I maintain that I'm wrong,
et cetera. That I would ever stutter
is out of the question. Altogether
credible and unaware of myself,
I think that I may rightfully claim
that I never contradict myself. I
am absent. I'm neither here nor th-th-th-there.

Hummel Hummel

Allerhand, wie sie abhebt,
bebend vor Energie,
wie sie aufsteigt,
sich, leise dröhnend,
dem Licht entgegen
gegen die Scheibe wirft.

Nach dem Absturz
ein neuer Versuch.
Geübter im Anflug,
mehr Umsicht, weniger Verve.
Zur Freiheit, zur Sonne.
Undurchdringlich das Glas.

Immer mattere Fühler,
aussichtslosere Touren.
Der Reinfall reine Routine.
Ein Leben für die Kunst.

Bis sie liegenbleibt,
schwach zuckend,
auf dem Fenstersims,
die pelzige Sängerin.

Humble-bee, Bumble-bee

Amazing, how she takes off
quivering with energy,
how she rises
and, softly thudding,
hurls herself towards light
against the window-pane.

After the crash,
another attempt,
more practised in the approach,
more caution, less vehemence.
To freedom, to the sun.
The glass remains impenetrable.

The antennae more and more limp,
hopeless sallies.
The fall mere routine.
A life for art's sake.

Till she just lies there,
faintly twitching,
on the window-sill,
that furry singer.

Paolo di Dono, genannt Uccello

Paolo di Dono, Sohn eines Baders,
verlor sich in einer neuen Wissenschaft,
einer neuen Zauberei: der Perspektive.
»So ermüdet er die Natur«, hieß es,
»bis der Geist sich füllt
mit Schwierigkeiten und ungelenk wird.«

Schlachten, Turniere. Die Krieger
undurchdringlich im Augenblick
vor dem Tod. Die Genauigkeit
im Ungewissen. Hasen, Windhunde,
Heuschrecken: Phantasmen
unter der Mondsichel,
im Orangenhain Wirbelstürme,
Hufe und Füße.

Einhörner auf den Wimpeln,
geflügelte Helme, hohe Hauben
aus Weidengeflecht, gepolstert
mit Haar, das Futter scharlachrot,
und eiserne Reiter,
von Schalmeien gehetzt,
auf gigantischen Holzpferden,
grün, weiß und rosa,
mit panischen Augen.

Jeder glaubt,
er sei der Mittelpunkt.
Nur der Maler nicht.
Er arbeitet »ruhig, sauber,
wie die Seidenraupe
an ihrem Faden«, arm,
unnütz, menschenscheu,
wild, »wirft er
die Zeit hinter die Zeit
und ermüdet die Natur«.

Paolo di Dono, known as Uccello

Paolo di Dono, a barber's son,
got lost in a new science,
a new sort of magic: perspective.
'He worries nature,' they said,
'until the mind is filled
with difficulties and grows awkward.'

Battles, tournaments. The fighters
impenetrable at the moment
before death. Precision
in uncertainty. Hares, greyhounds,
grasshoppers: phantasms
beneath the sickle moon,
in the orange grove whirlwinds,
hooves and feet.

Unicorns on the pennons,
winged helmets, tall hoods
of wickerwork, upholstered
with hair, the lining scarlet,
and iron horsemen
chased by shawms
on gigantic wooden horses,
green, white and pink,
with panic-stricken eyes.

Each one thinks
himself the centre.
All but the painter.
He works 'calmly, cleanly
like the silkworm
on its thread', poor,
useless, retiring,
wild, 'he casts
time behind time
and worries nature'.

Für Karajan und andere

Drei Männer in steifen Hüten
vor dem Kiewer Hauptbahnhof –
Posaune, Ziehharmonika, Saxophon –

im Dunst der Oktobernacht,
die zwischen zwei Zügen zaudert,
zwischen Katastrophe und Katastrophe:

vor Ermüdeten spielen sie, die voll Andacht
in ihre warmen Piroggen beißen
und warten, warten,

ergreifende Melodien, abgetragen
wie ihre Jacken und speckig
wie ihre Hüte, und wenn Sie da

fröstelnd gestanden wären unter Trinkern,
Veteranen, Taschendieben,
Sie hätten mir recht gegeben:

Salzburg, Bayreuth und die Scala
haben dem Bahnhof von Kiew
wenig, sehr wenig voraus.

For Karajan and Others

Three men in stiff hats
in front of Kiev Main Station –
trombone, accordion, saxophone –

in the vapours of an October night
that hesitates between two trains,
between disaster and disaster:

they play for tired people, who very devoutly
bite into their warm piroshki
and wait, wait,

heart-rending tunes, worn
like the jackets and greasy
as their hats, and if you

had stood there, chilled, among alcoholics,
veterans, pickpockets,
you would have agreed with me:

Salzburg, Bayreuth and La Scala
don't compare all that favourably
with the Main Station of Kiev.

Unschuldsvermutung

Diese Siebenjährige auf ihrem Trampolin,
wie sie mühelos und mit fliegenden Haaren
die Schwerkraft besiegt;

der Koch, der gespannt, den hölzernen Löffel im Mund,
leckt, lauscht, wartet, bis der Geschmack
hinter dem Geschmack durch seine Nüstern strömt;

der hoffnungslos verkannte Tonsetzer,
wie er mit affenartiger Lust
seine Kadenz in die Tasten hämmert;

das geistesabwesend inmitten von Spritzen und Bierdosen
auf der klammen Parkbank
ineinander vergrabene Paar;

der Mörder, der, außer sich vor Freude
über den idealen Elfmeter, seinen Auftrag,
sein Alibi, seinen Tatort vergißt;

oder auf ihrem Badetuch die blinzelnde dicke Alte da,
wie sie sich kratzt, wie sie entrückt
mit ihren sandigen Zehen spielt;

und der gebückte Schuhputzer, wie er sich sonnt
im Spiegel des Glanzes, den er mit seiner Spucke
auf die lederne Kappe gehext hat:

diese bis zur Bewußtlosigkeit glücklichen Lebewesen –
einen Augenblick lang können sie nichts dafür,
daß sie keine gewöhnlichen Tiere sind.

Presumption of Innocence

This seven-year-old girl on her trampoline,
how effortlessly, with her hair flying,
she gets the better of gravity;

the chef who, intent, the wooden spoon in his mouth,
licks, listens, waits for the flavour
behind the flavour to flow through his nostrils;

the hopelessly neglected tone-setter,
how with monkey-like relish
he hammers his cadenza into the keys;

the absent-minded couple in the midst of
syringes and beer cans on their clammy park bench
encased in each other;

the murderer who, beside himself with delight
at the ideal penalty-kick, forgets
his mission, his alibi, the place of the crime;

or the fat old woman over there who, blinking,
scratches herself, and ecstatically
plays with her sandy toes;

and the bent shoe-shine man, how he basks
in the reflection of the radiance which his saliva
has bewitched the leather toe-cap to yield:

these beings happy to the point of unconsciousness –
for a moment it isn't their fault
that they're no ordinary animals.

Das somnambule Ohr

Wie sollst du je wieder einschlafen,
wenn in der menschenleeren Stunde
ehe es hell wird,
das Haus klopft und scharrt,
wenn du es murmeln hörst
hinter der Wand?

Diese Schüsse, kommen sie aus einem Film,
den niemand sieht,
oder stirbt da einer im Treppenhaus?
Etwas gurrt, wo keine Taube lebt,
etwas ächzt – ein alter Kühlschrank
oder ein längst verschwundenes Liebespaar.

In den Ventilen zischt das Gas.
Es werden schwere Möbel gerückt.
Etwas tropft. Der Dampf tickt.
Das Wasser stürzt durch die Röhren.
Wer trinkt, wer duscht,
wer entleert sich da?

Und als es endlich still ist –
das Haus hält vor Angst die Luft an –,
vernimmst du ein Sirren,
fast jenseits des Hörbaren,
geisterhaft dünn wie der glitzernde Ring
eines unaufhaltsamen Zählers,

der sich im Dunkeln dreht.

The Somnambulist Ear

How will you ever get to sleep again
when in the hour empty of human sounds
before the first light
the house knocks and scratches,
when you hear it murmur
behind the wall?

These shots, do they come from a film
that nobody sees,
or is there someone dying on the staircase?
Something coos where no pigeon lives,
something sighs – an old refrigerator
or a pair of lovers long ago vanished?

In the vents the gas hisses.
Heavy furniture is shifted.
Something trickles. The steam ticks.
Water hurtles through the pipes.
Who's drinking, who's taking a shower?
Who's evacuating himself?

And when at last it's quiet –
the house holds its breath in terror –
you hear a whirring
almost beyond the audible,
phantasmally thin as the glittering ring
of an unstoppable meter

that revolves in the dark.

Klinische Meditation

Auf der Rolltreppe, am Strand, im Rasierspiegel:
überall Behinderte, Patienten, Pflegebedürftige,
doch niemand ist siech oder blöde. Ausgestorben
sind die Bresthaften. Keine Rede mehr
von Stockflüssen, Herzkuchen und Vapeurs.
Wo ist der Gelbe Brand geblieben,
der Englische Schweiß und die Mauke?
Auch die Plagen dauern nicht ewig.
Verschollene Schreckensworte: Hundstod,
Haarwurm und Häutige Bräune.
Rastlos sucht der Reaktor der Evolution
nach neuen Lösungen, neuen Geißeln.
Auch die Schäden verbessern sich,
von Jahr zu Jahr. Schlundpest und Blaue Rose
können nicht Schritt halten
mit fortschrittlicheren Erregern.
Keine Rote Liste trauert der Trommelsucht,
dem Drudenzopf und der Gnätze nach.
Triumphierend beugt sich die Wissenschaft
über das weißeste aller Betten
und murmelt ihr Totengebet.

Clinical Meditation

On the escalator, on the beach, in the shaving mirror:
everywhere the disabled, patients, people in need of care,
but no one is sick or demented. Obsolete
are the consumptives. No more talk
of chronic coryza, caked hearts and vapours.
What's become of the yellow gangrene?
Of the English malady and the scurvy?
Even afflictions don't last for ever.
Lost words that struck terror: dog's death,
hairworm and hymenoid brownness.
Restlessly the reactor of evolution looks
for new solutions, new hostages.
Even ailments improve
from year to year. The pharyngeal plague and blue erysipelas
can't keep pace
with progressive pathogens.
No red list mourns for tympanitis,
for the witches' braid or the scab.
Triumphantly science bends
over the whitest of beds
and mumbles its prayers for the dead.

Die Visite

Als ich aufsah von meinem leeren Blatt,
stand der Engel im Zimmer.

Ein ganz gemeiner Engel,
vermutlich unterste Charge.

Sie können sich gar nicht vorstellen,
sagte er, wie entbehrlich Sie sind.

Eine einzige unter fünfzehntausend Schattierungen
der Farbe Blau, sagte er,

fällt mehr ins Gewicht der Welt
als alles, was Sie tun oder lassen,

gar nicht zu reden vom Feldspat
und von der Großen Magellanschen Wolke.

Sogar der gemeine Froschlöffel, unscheinbar wie er ist,
hinterließe eine Lücke, Sie nicht.

Ich sah es an seinen hellen Augen, er hoffte
auf Widerspruch, auf ein langes Ringen.

Ich rührte mich nicht. Ich wartete,
bis er verschwunden war, schweigend.

The Visit

When I looked up from my blank page
there was an angel in the room.

A rather commonplace angel,
presumably of lower rank.

You cannot imagine, he said,
the degree to which you're dispensable.

Of the fifteen thousand hues of blue,
he said, each one makes more of a difference

than anything you may do
or refrain from doing,

not to mention the felspar
or the Great Magellanic Cloud.

Even the common plantain, unassuming
as it is, would leave a gap. Not you.

I could tell from his bright eyes –
he hoped for an argument, for a long fight.

I did not move. I waited in silence
until he had gone away.

Empfanger unbekannt – *Retour à l'expéditeur*

Vielen Dank für die Wolken.
Vielen Dank für das Wohltemperierte Klavier
und, warum nicht, für die warmen Winterstiefel.
Vielen Dank für mein sonderbares Gehirn
und für allerhand andre verborgne Organe,
für die Luft, und natürlich für den Bordeaux.
Herzlichen Dank dafür, daß mir das Feuerzeug nicht ausgeht,
und die Begierde, und das Bedauern, das inständige Bedauern.
Vielen Dank für die vier Jahreszeiten,
für die Zahl e und für das Koffein,
und natürlich für die Erdbeeren auf dem Teller,
gemalt von Chardin, sowie für den Schlaf,
für den Schlaf ganz besonders,
und, damit ich es nicht vergesse,
für den Anfang und das Ende
und die paar Minuten dazwischen
inständigen Dank,
meinetwegen für die Wühlmause draußen im Garten auch.

Addressee Unknown – *Retour à l'expéditeur*

Many thanks for the clouds.
Many thanks for the *Well-tempered Clavier*
and, why not, for the warm winter boots.
Many thanks for my strange brain
and for all manner of other hidden organs,
for the air, and, of course, for the claret.
Heartfelt thanks for my lighter and my desire
not running out of fuel,
as well as my regret, my deep regret.
Many thanks for the four seasons,
for the number e, for my dose of caffeine,
and, of course, for the strawberry dish
painted by Chardin, as well as for sleep,
for sleep quite especially, and,
last not least, for the beginning and the end
and the few minutes in between
fervent thanks,
even, if you like, for the voles out there in the garden.

Gedankenflucht (IV)

Die kleine Pilgerin da
auf ihrer chaotischen Bahn,
dieses umherirrende,
glimmende Nichts –
wie war doch der Name gleich? –
und was sucht sie nur,
die bis auf weiteres
unsterbliche Seele?

Sie wühlt im Müll,
unermüdlich, nach Weisheiten,
die plötzlich weg waren,
zerkrümelt in endlosen Permutationen,
vermoderten Paperbacks.

Sie kann nicht stillhalten,
will es nicht einsehen,
kann es einfach nicht fassen,
die winzige Wallfahrerin.

Wie sie sich faltet, dehnt,
faltet wie Blätterteig,
gewalkt von Energien
aus der Heliosphäre
und aus den tieferen Schichten
ihres Gehirns! Nein,

sie kann es nicht lassen,
vermischt sich, triebhaft,
nach alter Gewohnheit,
mit Wolken, Meeren, Gestirnen.

Bei dem, was der Fall ist,
bleibt es nicht. Ja,
sagt sie, ich will zurück,
ich will weiter, unabsehbar

Flight of Ideas (IV)

That little pilgrim there
on her chaotic course,
this rambling, groping,
glimmering nothing –
what did they say the name was? –
and what could it be looking for,
the provisionally
immortal soul?

She grubs in refuse,
indefatigably, for bits of wisdom
that suddenly were gone,
crumbled away in endless permutations,
in mouldy paperbacks.

She can't stay put,
won't see the point,
simply can't grasp it,
that tiny pilgrim.

How she folds up, expands,
folds up like puff pastry
rolled by energies
from the heliosphere
and from the deeper layers
of her brain! No,

she can't desist,
mingles, by instinct,
by old habit,
with clouds, oceans, stars.

Never is she content with
that which is the case.
Yes, she says, I want to go back,
I want to go on, to no known goal

bewege ich mich, bin bewegt,
bis auf weiteres bleibe ich,
in der Schwebe.

I move, I am moved,
for the time being, provisionally
I remain in suspense.

Die Grablegung

Eine sterbliche Hülle,
so heißt es,
aber was war drin?
Die Psyche,
sagen die Psychologen,
die Seele,
die Seelsorger,
die Persönlichkeit,
sagen die Personalchefs.

Dazu noch die Anima,
die Imago, der Dämon,
die Identität, das Ich,
das Es und das Überich.
Der Schmetterling,
der sich aus diesem Gedrängel
erheben soll,
gehört einer Art an,
von der wir nichts wissen.

The Entombment

Our mortal frame,
they call it.
But what did it hold?
The psychologist will say:
Your psyche.
Your soul,
the priest.
Your personality,
the personnel manager.

Furthermore,
there's the anima,
the imago, the daemon,
the identity and the Ego,
not to mention the Id
and the Super-Ego.

The butterfly which is to rise
from this very mixed lot
belongs to a species
about which nothing is known.

LIGHTER THAN AIR
LEICHTER ALS LUFT
(1999)

Optimistisches Liedchen

Hie und da kommt es vor,
daß einer um Hilfe schreit.
Schon springt ein andrer ins Wasser,
vollkommen kostenlos.

Mitten im dicksten Kapitalismus
kommt die schimmernde Feuerwehr
um die Ecke und löscht, oder im Hut
des Bettlers silbert es plötzlich.

Vormittags wimmelt es auf den Straßen
von Personen, die ohne gezücktes Messer
hin- und herlaufen, seelenruhig,
auf der Suche nach Milch und Radieschen.

Wie im tiefsten Frieden.

Ein herrlicher Anblick.

Optimistic Little Poem

Now and then it happens
that somebody shouts for help
and somebody else jumps in at once
and absolutely gratis.

Here in the thick of the grossest capitalism
round the corner comes the shining fire brigade
and extinguishes, or suddenly
there's silver in the beggar's hat.

Mornings the streets are full
of people hurrying here and there without
daggers in their hands, quite equably
after milk or radishes.

As though in a time of deepest peace.

A splendid sight.

Kriegserklärung

Im Hinterzimmer des Bierkellers,
wo sieben Besoffene sich versammelt haben,
fängt er an, der Krieg; er schwelt
in der Kinderkrippe; die Akademie
der Wissenschaften brütet ihn aus;
nein, in einem Kreißsaal von Gori
oder Braunau gedeiht er, im Internet,
in der Moschee; das kleine Gehirn
des patriotischen Dichters schwitzt ihn aus;
weil jemand beleidigt ist, weil jemand
Blut geleckt hat, in Gottes Namen,
wütet der Krieg, aus Gründen der Hautfarbe,
im Bunker, im Jux, oder aus Versehen;
weil Opfer gebracht werden müssen
für die Rettung der Menschheit, und zwar
besonders nachts, wegen der Ölfelder;
deshalb, weil auch die Selbstverstümmelung
ihren Reiz hat, und weil das Geld fließt,
fängt er an, der Krieg, im Delirium,
wegen des verlorenen Fußballspiels;
weit gefehlt, um Gottes willen; ja dann;
obwohl ihn niemand gewollt hat; aha;
nur so, zum Vergnügen, heldenhaft,
und weil uns nichts Besseres einfällt.

Explaining the Declaration

It starts in the pub, in the back room
where seven drunks are gathered together,
war; it smoulders
in the crèche; the Academy
of Sciences hatches it;
no, in a delivery room in Gori
or Braunau it flourishes, on the net,
in the mosque; it sweats
from the small brain of the patriotic poet;
because someone is offended, because someone
has tasted blood, in God's name,
war rages, on grounds of colour,
in the bunker, for a joke, or by mistake;
because there have to be sacrifices
to save mankind, and these
especially at night, because of the oilfields;
for this, that even self-mutilation
has its attractions and because there's money
war starts, in a delirium
because of a football match;
for no such thing, for heaven's sake; yes, then;
though nobody wanted it; aha;
just like that, for pleasure, heroically
and because we can't think of anything better to do.

Astrale Wissenschaft

Seine Welt aus fast nichts und nichts,
aus spukhaften Superstrings
im zehndimensionalen Raum,
Strangeness, Colour, Spin und Charm –

doch wenn er Zahnweh hat,
der Kosmologe;
wenn er in St Moritz
über die Piste stiebt;
Kartoffelsalat ißt
oder einer Dame beiwohnt,
die nicht an Bosonen glaubt;
wenn er stirbt,

verdunsten die mathematischen Märchen,
die Gleichungen schmelzen,
und er kehrt aus seinem Jenseits zurück
in die hiesige Welt
aus Schmerz, Schnee, Lust,
Kartoffelsalat und Tod.

Astral Science

His world of nearly nothing and nothing,
of ghostly superstrings
in ten-dimensional space,
strangeness, colour, spin and charm –

but when the cosmologist
has toothache;
when in St Moritz
he powders down the slopes;
eats potato salad
or sleeps with a lady
who does not believe in bosons;
when he dies

the mathematical fairytales evaporate,
the equations melt
and he comes back out of the beyond
into this world here
of pain, snow, pleasure,
potato salad and death.

Das Einfache, das schwer zu erfinden ist

Nichts gegen den Mikroprozessor,
aber wie stünden wir da
ohne das Wasser?
Was ist schon eine Jupitersonde,
verglichen mit dem Gehirn einer Fliege?
Wie sie sich abmühen,
diese Labormäuse, mit dem Klonen!
Doch vorzüglicher ist es, zu vögeln.
Und der Löwenzahn erst,
wie der es macht: heitere,
unübertroffene Eleganz!
Nie im Leben,
liebe Nobelpreisträger,
gebt es nur zu,
hättet ihr sowas erfunden.

The Simple Thing Hard to Invent

Nothing against the microprocessor
but where would we be
without water?
Even a Jupiter probe
what is it
compared with the brain of a fly?
Those laboratory mice
labouring at cloning!
Fucking is a finer thing.
Go no further than the dandelion,
the way it does it: serene
unrivalled elegance.
Never in your lives
my dear Nobel Prizewinners
admit it
would you ever have invented anything like that.

Ein schwarzer Tag

An solchen Donnerstagen
hackt sogar der erfahrenste Metzger
sich einen Finger ab.
Alle Züge haben Verspätung,
weil sich die Selbstmörder
nicht mehr beherrschen können.
Der Zentralcomputer im Pentagon
ist schon lange zusammengebrochen,
und alle Wiederbelebungsversuche
in den Freibädern kommen zu spät.

Zu allem Überfluß
kocht nebenan bei Marotzkes
jetzt auch noch die Milch über,
der Hund hat Verdauungsbeschwerden,
und nicht einmal Tante Olga,
die Unverwüstliche,
ist so ganz auf der Höhe.

A Black Day

On Thursdays like this one
even the most experienced butcher
chops his finger off.
All the trains are late
because the suicidal
have finally let go.
The central computer in the Pentagon
crashed early on
and at the swimming baths
efforts at resucitation are all too late.

And as if that weren't enough
next door at Mrs Marotzke's
now the milk is boiling over,
the dog has something wrong with its digestion
and not even Aunty Olga,
the Indestructible,
is quite tip-top.

Weltmarkt

Was wir jetzt brauchen, ist eine Schruppscheibe
ein Trimmerkopf, eine Schnittstellenkarte,
eingeflogen aus Japan. Plötzlich
sind Souvenirs aus Timbuktu da,
Ikonen, geraubte Säuglinge. Überall
ein und dieselben Rasierklingen,
Kongreßteilnehmer und Killerbienen.
Autobomben kursieren, Frauen
aus dem Versandkatalog landen,
Konten bewegen sich via Satellit.
Ganz neue Viren schweben ein.
Nur ab und zu liegt am Straßenrand
ein Bettler da, der sich nicht rührt.

World Market

What we need now is a sander,
a trimmer head, an interface card
flown in from Japan. Suddenly
there are souvenirs from Timbuktu,
icons, kidnapped babies. Everywhere
the same razorblades, the same
people at conferences and killer bees.
Car bombs do the rounds, wives
land from the catalogues,
bank accounts shift by satellite.
Brand new viruses come floating in.
Only now and then by the roadside
there's a beggar lying, motionless.

Arme Kassandra

Sie war die einzige, die es kommen sah,
sie ganz allein: das alles, sagte sie,
werde bös enden. Natürlich
hat ihr kein Mensch geglaubt.
Sagenhaft lange her. Aber seitdem
sagen es alle. Ein Blick genügt,
auf die Börsenkurse, den Stau
und die Spätnachrichten. Fragt sich nur,
was »das alles« bedeutet, und *wann?*
Bis dahin natürlich glaubt,
was alle sagen, kein Mensch.
Ein Blick genügt, auf die Zweitwagen,
die Biergärten und die Heiratsanzeigen.

Poor Cassandra

She was the only one who saw it coming,
just her: all this, she said,
will end badly. Of course
not a soul believed her.
A long long time ago. Now
everyone is saying it. Look
at the share index, the traffic jams
and the late-night news. The only question is
what 'all this' means, and *when?*
Till then of course
not a soul believes what everyone is saying.
Look at the second cars,
the beer gardens and the marriage announcements.

Fehler

Nebenan spielt ein Kind *Pour Elise*.
Man hört den Fehler, immer wieder von vorn.
Das Dogma von der Unfehlbarkeit
war ein Fauxpas. Es ist ein fataler Patzer
des Parasiten, den Wirt zu töten.
Man nennt das auch *Globalisierung*.

Schamhaft verbirgt sich der entscheidende Fehler
in einer Düne von geringfügigen Irrtümern
und geht darin unter. An warnenden Stimmen
hat es noch nie gefehlt, die sagen:
Die Welt ist das Unkorrigierbare.

Rührende Reparaturversuche, Flicken,
Plomben, Reformen, Verbesserungen
mit roter Tinte und Pentimenti
führen zu vollkommen neuen Schnitzern.

Gewiß, Geburtsfehler und Fehlgeburten,
das sind zwei Paar Stiefel.
Doch auch die Leistung geht fehl,
die Farbe, die Bitte, der Start,
der Tritt und die Zündung.

Eine Milchstraße von Verirrungen,
die wundernimmt. Aufs Ganze gesehen,
entsteht daraus ein Mirakel.

Fehler um jeden Preis zu vermeiden,
das wäre verfehlt.
Man gesteht ja, räumt ein,
daß man sich vertan hat,
verschrieben, verrannt.

Eror

Next door a child is playing *Für Elise*.
You can hear the wrong notes,
over and over again.
The Dogma of Infallibility
was a faux-pas. It's a fatal mistake
on the part of the parasite
to kill the host. Nowadays
they call it *globalisation*.

Bashfully, the crucial error
hides in an avalanche of tiny slips
and gets lost in it. There has never been
a dearth of warning voices
proclaiming the universe incorrigible.

Rather touching, all our attempts
to repair it, patch it up
and improve on it:
fillings, reforms, proof corrections
with red ink and pentimenti,
resulting in brand new aberrations.

A miscarriage and a congenital defect
are worlds apart.
False starts, misfires,
foul jumps and Freudian slips –

a galaxy of aberrations!
Strange enough how they add up
to a miracle of sorts.

To avoid mistakes at any cost
would be wrong. We concede,
admit, confess that there have been
certain slips, howlers, goofs and gaffes.

Manche Gedichte zum Beispiel
wären vollkommen,
hätte sie vor diesem Los
nicht ein winziger Fehler bewahrt.

Aus Versehen ist man glücklich,
zuweilen, einen Moment lang,
aus Versehen. Aber etwas feit.

Some poems, for example,
might have been perfect,
had not a slight oversight
come to their rescue.

Our moment of bliss comes about
inadvertently, by a fluke.
But something is always amiss.

Prästabilierte Disharmonie

Für jeden, der seine Bierflasche
auf dem Kopf des Tamilen zertrümmert
ein Chirurg in der Notaufnahme,
der den Schädel zusammenflickt.
Und umgekehrt.

Für jeden Minensucher,
der seine Haut riskiert,
ein Waffenhändler.
Und umgekehrt.

Für jeden Vergewaltiger eine Frau
mit dem Steakmesser in der Hand,
für jeden Sozialarbeiter ein Neonazi,
für jeden Besserverdienenden
ein Steuerfahnder, für jedes Monster
eine sanfte Madonna, und umgekehrt.

Ach, alle Hände voll zu tun
hat ein jeder von uns.
Da ist kein Ende in Sicht.

Pre-established Disharmony

For every man smashing his beer bottle
on the asylum-seeker's head
a surgeon in casualty
patching it up.
And vice versa.

For every mine-clearer
risking life and limb
an arms-dealer.
And vice versa.

For every rapist a woman
with the carving knife in her hand,
for every social worker a neo-Nazi,
for everyone in a higher income bracket
a tax investigator, for every monster
a gentle madonna, and vice versa.

Oh, every one of us
has his hands full.
There is no end in sight.

Leichter als Luft

Besonders schwer
wiegen Gedichte nicht.
Solange der Tennisball steigt,
ist er, glaube ich,
leichter als Luft.

Das Helium sowieso,
die Eingebung, dieses Kribbeln
in unserm Gehirn,
auch das Elmsfeuer
und die natürlichen Zahlen.

Sie wiegen so gut wie nichts,
von den transzendenten,
ihren vornehmen Vettern,
obwohl sie zahllos sind,
gar nicht zu reden.

Soviel ich weiß, gilt das auch
für den Strahlenkranz des Magneten,
den wir nicht sehen,
für die meisten Heiligenscheine
und für ausnahmslos alle Walzerklänge.

Leichter als Luft,
wie der vergessene Kummer
und der bläuliche Rauch
der endgültig letzten Zigarette,
ist natürlich das Ich,

und, soviel ich weiß,
steigt der Geruch des Brandopfers,
der den Göttern so wohlgefällig ist,
immer gen Himmel.
Der Zeppelin auch.

Lighter Than Air

Poems
do not weigh all that much.
As long as the tennis ball is climbing
it is, I believe,
lighter than air.

Helium for sure,
inspiration,
that tickling in the brain,
also St Elmo's fire
and natural numbers.

They weigh nearly nothing
and less still
their posh cousins
the transcendental numbers
even though innumerable.

So far as I know
that is also true of the field around a magnet
which we cannot see,
for most haloes
and for all the tunes of waltzes without exception.

Lighter than air
like forgotten grief
and the bluish smoke
of the definitely last cigarette
is of course the first person

and, so far as I know,
the scent of burnt offerings
pleasing to the gods
always rises towards the heavens.
As does a zeppelin.

Vieles bleibt ohnehin
in der Schwebe.
Am leichtesten wiegt vielleicht,
was von uns übrigbleibt,
wenn wir unter der Erde sind.

Much in any case
hangs in the balance.
Least of all perhaps
weighs what remains of us
when we are under the ground.

Grünes Madrigal

Plutonium und Beton –
natürlich gewinnen die Pflanzen
immer, im großen und ganzen.

Schon lauert in den Büros,
siehe, das fleißige Lieschen,
draußen das wilde Radieschen.

Die Gräser, wie unverschämt
sie jede Autobahn sprengen,
wuchern und wühlen und drängen!

O Siemens, vergiß es doch.
Über die Kernreaktoren
siegen zuletzt nur die Sporen.

Was heißt schon Becquerel, CO_2,
Kryptogamen fühlen sich wohl dabei.
Rührend, die Sorge ums Knabenkraut.
Was ist mit unserer eignen Haut?

Green Madrigal

Plutonium and concrete –
by and large, naturally
plants are the winners, always will be.

Lurking already in the office
behold: Busy Lizzy
and outside: cow parsley.

And the grasses, how shamelessly
they explode every motorway,
rampant, insistent, burrowing away.

O Siemens, forget it!
Over the nuclear reactors
spores in the end will be the victors.

All the talk about becquerels and CO_2:
cryptogams do very nicely, thank you.
Wild orchids: sweet, the way we fuss.
But what about us?

Geräusche

Endlich Ruhe, jetzt, wo sie alle schlafen,
die dröhnenden Fußballfans,
Biker, Besoffene, Dealer.
Nur ganz fern, unsichtbar,
am Neonhimmel,
schnattert ein Rettungshubschrauber.
Aber dann hörst du diesen Tropfen –
was kann es sein, das da tropft
und tropft? Ein technisches Sirren
ist im Beton, etwas Flüssiges
rieselt schwach, es knackt im Ohr,
in den Gelenken, leise faucht
die Luft in deinen Lungen,
Ströme knistern im Haar,
geisterhaft, und je mehr du lauschst,
desto deutlicher vernimmst du
jenseitige Frequenzen, es ist,
um verrückt zu werden!
Du hältst dir die Ohren zu,
vergeblich. Dann aber, kaum
läßt du die Hände sinken –
horch! Es regt sich nichts mehr,
nirgends. Das Nichts regt sich.
Panische Stille.

Noises

Peace and quiet at last, now they're all asleep
the yowling fans
the bikers, drunks, dealers.
Only very distant and invisible
on the neon sky
the racket of a rescue helicopter.
But then you hear the drip.
What can it be that is dripping
and dripping? There's a mechanical humming
in the concrete, something fluid
is trickling faintly, cracklings in your ears
and joints, the air hisses
softly in your lungs
ghostly currents crepitate in your hair
and the more you listen
the clearer you hear
frequencies from beyond, enough
to drive you mad.
You stop your ears
in vain. But then
no sooner do you remove your hands –
hark! There's nothing stirring any more,
nowhere. There is Nothing, stirring.
Silence, stillness, panic.

Leisere Töne

Immer nur die Dosis steigern,
ganz verkehrt. Vorübergehend
das meiste beiseite lassen –
auch nicht schlecht: weichere Wörter,
weniger Krach in der Lyrik
und im Verbrauchermarkt.

Möglicherweise kommt sie ja noch,
die blaue Stunde, vorübergehend,
bevor der nächste Versager beginnt,
in die Menge zu feuern.

Flaumige Sachen, adagio,
bis zur Gedankenlosigkeit aufmerksam
an etwas Nachgiebiges rühren,
an einen Mundwinkel oder ein Moos.
Überhaupt, auf die geringfügigeren Gefühle
ist am ehesten noch Verlaß.

A Softer Voice

To increase the daily dose
will do you no good.
Let most of what's going on pass
and you'll be better off.
Softer words, less of a racket
in poetry and in shopping malls.

Maybe some blue hour
is still awaiting you,
the moment before the next nitwit
will open fire on all passers-by.

Downy things, adagio, aware
to the point where your mind goes blank,
touching a cushion of moss
or the corner of a yielding mouth.
Most likely, of all your feelings
the most trustworthy are the minor ones.

Unpolitische Vorlieben

Dieses kleine Lächeln der Cellistin
nach der Kadenz im zweiten Satz,
obwohl soeben der Sicherheitsrat
zusammengetreten ist;

der tiefe Ernst, mit dem sich die Frau dort
in den Trümmern ihrer Wohnküche schminkt,
obwohl im Regierungsviertel
noch immer geschossen wird;

der Ehekrach dieser Achtzigjährigen,
wegen der Katzenhaare im Bett,
obwohl die Friedensverhandlungen
die entscheidende Phase erreicht haben;

das heulende Elend wegen der Jubiläumstasse,
die das Dienstmädchen zerschmettert hat,
obwohl der Währungsfonds im selben Moment
den Beistandskredit verweigert;

und hinter der Scheune das Liebespaar,
vor Eifer besinnungs- und atemlos,

obwohl

Unpolitical Preferences

That little smile on the cellist's face
after her cadenza in the second movement
even though the Security Council
has just convened;

the deep seriousness with which the woman there
puts on her make-up in the ruins of her kitchen dining-room
even though around the government buildings
there is still firing;

that man and wife, octogenarians, rowing
about cat hairs in the bed
even though peace negotiations
have reached a decisive phase;

the howls of grief because the maid
has smashed the Jubilee mug
even though the Monetary Fund at that very moment
has refused credit support;

and behind the barn the lovers
breathless and beside themselves with eagerness

even though

Analgeticum

Vollkommen schmerzlos –
das kann eine Stunde dauern
oder ein paar Jahrzehnte lang,
je nachdem. Glück gehabt,
vorübergehend, obwohl...
Das Glück, dieses riesige,
unvermeidliche Aspirin –
Nebenwirkungen: keine –,
es grenzt an Gleichgültigkeit.
Das tut gut, obwohl,
wer da vorübergeht,
immer so schmerzlos,
spürt immer weniger.

Analgesic

Quite without pain –
it may last an hour
or a few decades
depending. Lucky
for now, happy enough
to be going on with although...
Happiness, the vast
inevitable aspirin –
side-effects: none –
it verges on apathy.
Feels better although
a man going on
always so painlessly
feels less and less.

Aus freien Stücken

»Ich liebe Teerosen«, sagst du, Gevatter,
»aber ein satter Verlustvortrag
ist auch nicht zu verachten.«
»Ich brauchte einen Vibrator«,
sagt deine Frau, »und du schenkst mir
eine Erstausgabe von Nietzsche.«

So etwas hört man öfters.
Doch nicht jeder hat, wie du,
Genosse, die Qual der Wahl
zwischen einer Kiste Lafite
und einem Urlaub auf den Seychellen.
Leicht gesagt, Willensfreiheit.

Buridans Esel mußte verhungern.
Auch zuviel Heu, Brüderchen,
macht nicht unbedingt glücklich.
Zwischen Bolschewismus und Golf,
Dollar und Yen, Nike und Adidas
hin- und hergerissen, Kollege,

bist du, schwankendes Rohr.
Also, Sportsfreund, was ist?
Fährst du nun an den Baum
mit deiner 1200er BMW,
oder setzt du dir gleich
den Goldenen Schuß?

Schwerwiegende Entschlüsse,
kaum zu fassen, mein Lieber!
Greif zum Pendel,
frage den Analytiker,
erforsche den Kaffeesatz,
damit du weißt, was du willst.

Of His Own Free Will

'I love tea roses,' so you say, my friend,
'but a fat loss carried forward
is no bad thing either.'
'I could do with a vibrator,'
says your wife, 'and you give me
a first edition of Nietzsche.'

You hear it all the time.
But not everyone has, as you do,
comrade, the torment of choosing
between a case of Lafite
and a holiday on the Seychelles.
Not so easy, having free will.

Buridan's ass died of hunger.
Too much hay won't necessarily
make you a happy man, chum.
Between bolshevism and golf,
dollar and yen, Nike and Adidas
torn hither and thither, colleague

you're a reed in the wind. Come now,
sportsman, what shall it be?
Drive into a tree
in your BMW
or without more ado
OD? My dear chap

these are decisions
almost too weighty to take.
Play pendulum
ask your analyst
study the tea-leaves, and so
find out what you want.

Warnung vor der Gerechtigkeit

Sie glauben also im Ernst,
Sie wären zu kurz gekommen.
Ungerecht, behaupten Sie,
hätte die Welt Sie behandelt?
Dabei sehen wir doch,
wie emsig Sie ohne Krücken
tippeln, in Ihrem Alter,
und nachts versinken Sie
in eine Dame, die Sie erträgt!

Womit haben Sie es verdient,
unter einem höheren Himmel
als Ihr Hündchen zu wandeln?
Als ob Ihnen zustünde,
was Sie alles verschlingen,
wenn der Tag lang ist,
zum Beispiel die Luft!

Wir warnen Sie! Nicht auszudenken,
was Ihnen zuteil würde,
ginge's mit rechten Dingen zu.
Das Beste nämlich fällt uns
umsonst in Schoß und Mund –
Ihnen auch! –, warum und woher
weiß niemand, launisch,
Gerechten und Ungerechten,
manchmal wie Manna im Sand.

Beware of Justice

So you honestly think
you have not had your due?
The world, you insist,
has treated you unfairly?
And yet we observe
how busily without crutches
at your age you trot along
and sink every night
into a lady who can bear you.

Why should you go your ways
under a higher heaven than your doggie does?
What have you done to deserve it?
As if it was yours by right
all the stuff you consume
on a long day –
air, for example.

Be warned. It doesn't bear thinking about
what would be dealt you
if you were dealt with fairly.
The best things fall in our laps
and our mouths – in yours too –
for free and why and where from
nobody knows, they fall by a whim
to the just and the unjust
sometimes like manna in the sand.

An einen Ratsuchenden

Aromatherapie, Eheberatung, Diät
oder *Mensch ärgere dich nicht* spielen,
an der Pforte des Trappistenklosters läuten
und ein neues Leben anfangen,
das ist auch keine Lösung.
Das Zweitstudium hast du hinter dir,
und in Tibet warst du auch schon einmal.
Einmal ist keinmal, glaubst du.
Nur zu, alter Esel! Uns aber
bleibst du bitte vom Leib
mit deinem Gewinsel.
Auf so einen wie dich
können wir nämlich verzichten.

To One Seeking Counsel

Aromatherapy, marriage guidance, diet
or play Ludo,
ring at the gate of the Trappist monastery
and start a new life
that's no answer either.
You've been back to college once already
and once already you've been to Tibet.
But once doesn't count, in your view.
Get on with it, you old fool. But
leave us in peace, will you
spare us your whining.
We can do without
types like you.

Gegebenenfalls

Wähle unter den Fehlern,
die dir gegeben sind,
aber wähle richtig.
Vielleicht ist es falsch,
das Richtige
im falschen Moment
zu tun, oder richtig,
das Falsche
im richtigen Augenblick?
Ein Schritt daneben,
nicht wieder gut zu machen.
Der richtige Fehler,
einmal versäumt,
kehrt nicht so leicht wieder.

Should the Occasion Arise

Choose among the errors
given to you
but choose right.
Might it not be wrong
to do the right thing
at the wrong moment
or right
to do the wrong
at the right moment?
One false step
never to be made good.
The right error
should you miss it
may never come again.

Tagesordnung

Steuerberater anrufen, arbeiten auch.
Brüten über dem Foto einer Frau,
die sich umgebracht hat.
Nachschlagen, wann das Wort *Feindbild*
zum ersten Mal aufgetaucht ist.
Nach dem Donner die Blasen betrachten,
die der Wolkenbruch auf das Pflaster wirft,
und die nasse Luft trinken.
Rauchen auch, ohne Ton fernsehen.
Sich fragen, woher das sexuelle Kribbeln
mitten in einer öden Sitzung kommt.
Sieben Minuten lang an Algerien denken.
Hemmungslos wie ein Zwölfjähriger fluchen
über einen abgebrochenen Fingernagel.
Sich an einen bestimmten Abend erinnern,
vor einundzwanzig Jahren, im Juni,
ein schwarzer Pianist spielte cha cha cha,
und jemand weinte vor Zorn.
Zahnpasta kaufen nicht vergessen.
Rätseln, warum $e^{\pi i} = -1$;
warum Gott die Menschen niemals
in Ruhe läßt, umgekehrt auch nicht.
Glühbirne in der Küche auswechseln.
Die leblose, feuchte, zerraufte Krähe
spitzfingrig vom Balkon holen.
Den Wolken zusehen, den Wolken.
Schlafen auch, schlafen.

Order of the Day

Ring the accountant, also do some work.
Brood over the photograph of a woman
who has killed herself.
Look up when the word *Feindbild*
first appeared.
After the thunder contemplate the bubbles
flung down on the street by the cloudburst
and drink in the wet air.
Cigarettes too, and watch television with the sound off.
Wonder where, in the middle of a desolate meeting,
the itch of sex comes from.
Think about Algeria for seven minutes.
Let go and swear like a twelve-year-old
over a broken fingernail.
Remember a particular evening
twenty-one years ago, in June,
a black pianist was playing cha cha
and somebody was weeping with rage.
Remember to buy toothpaste.
Ponder why $e^{\pi i} = -1$;
why God will not leave Man
in peace, and vice versa.
Change a lightbulb in the kitchen.
Fetch the lifeless, damp, bedraggled crow
off the balcony with the tips of the fingers.
Watch the clouds, the clouds.
Sleep too, sleep.

Zugunsten der Versäumnisse

Ungelesene Klassiker, Erfindungen,
die er sich und andern erspart hat,
verlorene Wetten,
Pistolen mit Ladehemmung,
Titel, Posten, Orden,
die er sich entgehen ließ,
in letzter Minute verpaßte Flugzeuge,
unvergeßliche Flops, schäbige Siege,
an denen er haarscharf vorbei
geschliddert ist, und Frauen,
mit denen er nie ins Bett ging:

In seinem Rollstuhl gedenkt er
all dessen, was er vermieden,
womit er die Welt verschont hat,
dankbar und zärtlich.

In Praise of Sins of Omission

Unread classics, inventions
he has spared himself and others,
lost wagers
jammed pistols
titles, positions, honours
he let pass by,
aeroplanes missed at the last minute
unforgettable flops, shabby triumphs
he escaped by a hair's breadth
and women he never went to bed with.

In his wheelchair
he remembers with gratitude and affection
all the things he has avoided
and allowed the world to do without.

Eine zarte Regung

Mein Großvater,
dieser Glückliche,
verstand wenig vom Leben.
Er keuchte vor Appetit,
trug flotte Hüte
und glaubte häufig,
er wäre im Recht.
Mit siebenundneunzig
sah er, ungläubig
und zum erstenmal,
eine Klinik von innen.
»Schade«, murmelte er,
»hätte ich nur gewußt,
wie reizend sie sind,
die jungen Schwestern
an meinem Bett,
wie sanft ihre Hände,
früher, viel früher
wäre ich krank geworden«,
verzog die Mundwinkel,
wandte die Augen
zur Klingel und starb.

Tender Stirrings

My grandfather
happy man
never got far in thinking about life.
He panted with appetite,
wore natty hats
and frequently
thought he was in the right.
At ninety-seven
incredulous
and for the first time
he saw the inside of a hospital.
'Pity,' he murmured
'if only I'd known
how charming the young nurses are
around my bed
how gentle their hands
sooner, much sooner
I'd have fallen ill.'
He pulled a face
turned his eyes
to the bell, and died.

Eingeständnis

Neuerdings ertappe ich mich dabei
zu bewundern. Eine Angewohnheit,
als die Wut süßer
und gefährlicher als das Rauchen.
Den Mann, der von zwei Eiern lebt,
ein weiches am Morgen,
am Abend ein Rührei,
und mehr – sagt er – braucht er nicht;
den Chinesen, der mutterseelenallein
an der böhmischen Grenze
seinen *Lotus-Garten* eröffnet;
den Lektor, der tagaus tagein
hoffnungslos Sätze verbessert;
die sechsmal geliftete Gattin;
den Bankräuber, den Disc-Jockey,
den Politiker in seiner Vollzugsanstalt
und den Penner in seinem Tütenkral:
Unermüdliche sind es, ohne Warum
hingegeben wie der fleißige Maulwurf
und die bescheidene Ameise
ihrem rätselhaften Werk.
Immer schwerer gelingen mir
Haß, Neid und Verachtung,
diese jugendlichen Gefühle.
Ein Zeichen von Schwäche.
Mein heimliches Laster gefällt mir.
Ja, ich bewundere sie, fast alle,
Verlierer, unaufhaltsame,
wie sie tasten und wühlen.

Confession

Lately I've caught myself
admiring. A habit
sweeter than rage
and more dangerous than smoking.
That man who lives off two eggs
one soft-boiled in the morning
in the evening one scrambled
and more than that – he says – he does not need;
the Chinaman all alone in the world
on the Bohemian border
opening his *Lotus Garden*;
the editor, day in, day out,
hopelessly correcting sentences;
that wife with her six face-lifts;
the bankrobber, the disc jockey,
the politician in his prison
and the dosser in his kraal of plastic bags:
they are indefatigable, without why and wherefore
devoted like the diligent mole
and the humble ant
to their mysterious work.
Harder and harder for me
are hatred, envy, contempt
the youthful feelings.
A sign of weakness.
I like my secret vice.
Yes, I admire them, almost all of them,
losers, unstoppably
feeling their way and burrowing.

Grenzen der Vorstellungskraft

Zuviel verlangt, daß du begreifst,
was die Zahl 9 hoch 17 hoch 17 bedeutet,
daß du weißt, wie dem andern zumute ist,
wenn er Zahnweh hat,
daß du an die Erdbebenopfer denkst,
wenn du Jetztjetztjetzt bist
bei deiner Freundin im Bett
und sonst gar nichts.
Analphabet der Armut,
solange du Geld hast,
und als armes Schwein
ahnst du nichts von den schweren Sorgen
der Milliardäre. Ewiger Inländer,
verbannt ins eigene Nest,
kannst du nicht mitreden.
Liebe erste Person Singular,
du Ausbund von Phantasielosigkeit –
versuche dir vorzustellen,
wie du dem Virus schmeckst,
der in deiner Lunge haust,
wie die Katze dich sieht
oder irgendein Gott.
Stell dir vor, winziger Kiesel,
wie du im Wasser versinkst
und über dir schließt sich
der Spiegel der Welt
spurlos und glatt.
Aber das kannst du nicht.

Limits of the Imagination

It's asking too much that you comprehend
what 9 to the power of 17 to the power of 17 means
that you know what someone else feels like
with toothache
that you think of the earthquake victims
when you are now now now
with your girl in bed
and are nothing else.
Illiterate in poverty
so long as you have money
and skint you have
no inkling of the weighty anxieties
of millionaires. Eternal native
banished to your own nest
you have no say.
Love in the first person singular
prodigiously lacking in imagination
try to imagine
what you taste like to the virus
housing in your lungs
or how the cat or any
god sees you.
Imagine, tiny pebble,
you sink in the water
and over you closes
the surface of the world
smoothly and with no trace of you.
But you can't imagine it.

Die Große Göttin

Sie flickt und flickt,
über ihr zerbrochenes Stopfei gebeugt,
ein Fadenende zwischen den Lippen.
Tag und Nacht flickt sie.
Immer neue Laufmaschen, neue Löcher.

Manchmal nickt sie ein,
nur einen Augenblick,
ein Jahrhundert lang.
Mit einem Ruck wacht sie auf
und flickt und flickt.

Wie klein sie geworden ist,
klein, blind und runzlig!
Mit ihrem Fingerhut tastet sie
nach den Löchern der Welt
und flickt und flickt.

The Great Goddess

She works away day and night,
bent over her darning-egg,
an end of thread between her lips,
mending all manner of things.
Ever new holes, new ladders.

Sometimes she nods off
just for a moment
or for a century. Then,
pulling herself together,
she is back at her needlework.

How tiny she has become,
tiny, wrinkled and blind!
With her thimble she feels
for the holes in the world
and darns and darns.

A HISTORY OF CLOUDS
DIE GESCHICHTE DER WOLKEN
(2003)

Die Geschichte der Wolken

1

So wie sie auftauchen, über Nacht
oder aus heiterem Himmel,
kann man kaum behaupten,
daß sie geboren werden.
So wie sie unmerklich vergehen,
haben sie keine Ahnung vom Sterben.
Ihrer Vergänglichkeit kann sowieso
keiner das Wasser reichen.

Majestätisch einsam und weiß
steigen sie auf vor seidigem Blau,
oder drängeln sich aneinander
wie frierende Tiere, kollektiv
und dumpf, ballen sich tintig
zu elektrischen Katastrophen,
dröhnen, leuchten, ungerührt,
hageln und schütten sich aus.

Dann wieder prahlen sie
mit eitlen Künsten, verfärben sich,
äffen alles, was fest ist, nach.
Ein Spiel ist ihre Geschichte,
unblutig, älter als unsre.
Historiker, Henker und Ärzte
brauchen sie nicht, kommen aus
ohne Häuptlinge, ohne Schlachten.

Ihre hohen Wanderungen
sind ruhig und unaufhaltsam.
Es kümmert sie nichts.
Wahrscheinlich glauben sie
an die Auferstehung, gedankenlos
glücklich wie ich, der ihnen
auf dem Rücken liegend
eine Weile lang zusieht.

A History of Clouds

1

Appearing as they do,
overnight, or out of the blue,
they can hardly be considered
as being born.
Passing away imperceptibly
they have no notion of dying.
And anyway, nobody
can match their transience.

Majestically lonely and white
they rise against a silky blue
or huddle together,
like animals in the cold, collectively
and numb, cluster to form
ink-dark electric disasters,
boom and flash, unmoved,
let hail and water fall.

Then again they boast
of vain feats, change colour,
ape all that is solid.
A game is their history,
unbloodied, older than ours.
They don't need historians,
henchmen, medics, make do
without chiefs, without battles.

Their wanderings high up
are quiet and inexorable.
Nothing bothers them.
Probably they believe
in resurrection, thoughtlessly
happy like me,
lying on my back and
watching them for a while.

2

Gegen Streß, Kummer, Eifersucht, Depression
empfiehlt sich die Betrachtung der Wolken.
Mit ihren rotgoldenen Abendrändern
übertreffen sie Patinir und Tiepolo.
Die flüchtigsten aller Meisterwerke,
schwerer zu zählen als jede Rentierherde,
enden in keinem Museum.

Wolkenarchäologie – eine Wissenschaft
für die Engel. Ja, ohne die Wolken
stürbe alles, was lebt. Erfinder sind sie:
Kein Feuer ohne sie, kein elektrisches Licht.
Ja, es empfiehlt sich, bei Müdigkeit,
Wut und Verzweiflung, die Augen
gen Himmel zu wenden.

3

Der blaue Himmel ist blau.
Damit ist alles gesagt
über den blauen Himmel.

Dagegen diese fliegenden Bilderrätsel –
obwohl die Lösung immerfort wechselt,
kann sie ein jeder entziffern.

Unfaßbar sind sie in höheren Lagen,
nebulös. Und wie sanft
sie hinsterben! So schmerzlos

ist wenig hier. Die Wolken,
sie haben keine Angst, als wüßten sie,
daß sie immer wieder zur Welt kommen.

2

In case of stress, grief, jealousy, depression
cloud-watching is recommended.
With their red and golden evening borders
they surpass Patinir and Tiepolo.
The most fleeting of all masterworks,
harder to count than any herd of reindeer,
don't end up in any museum.

Archaeology of clouds – a science
for the angels. Yes, without clouds
everything living would die. They are inventors:
No fire without them, no electric light.
Indeed, in exhaustion, anger and despair
it is recommended that the eyes
be turned to the sky.

3

The blue sky is blue.
That says everything
about the blue sky.

These flying rebuses however –
although the answer changes all the time,
anyone can decipher them.

They are intangible, so high above,
nebulous. And the gentleness
of their dying! So painless

few things here can match it. The clouds
have no fear, as if they knew:
they'll come into this world again and again.

4

Wie sie sich seidig hinzieht, diese Population
von glänzenden Rippen, Flocken und Schleiern,
wie sie sich eilig aufbauschen, diese Bänke,
Ballen, Walzen, Kuppeln, Türme, wie dann wieder
alles stockt, wochenlang hängenbleibt,
grau und verdrießlich – Fortschritte
werden nicht gemacht in der Evolution
der Wolken. Vom Kampf ums Dasein
gar keine Spur! Eine Prise Staub genügt,
ein bißchen Salz oder Rauch. Dann dampft man,
entlädt sich, blitzt und hagelt und schneit.
Ja, sie mutieren unentwegt, über Nacht,
diese Kreaturen, gewaltlos und einfallsreich.
Variationen noch und noch, und bei alledem
bleibt alles beim alten.

5

Aber sie können auch anders.
Und dann, aus Wut oder Übermut
ballen sie sich, und faustdick
drohen sie. Schwarzgallig knallend
bricht aus ihnen die alte Gewalt.
Plötzlich platzt alles, Schall,
Spannung, Wasser und Eis.

Dann flüchten wir, wie immer
im Bett überrascht, auf die Dächer,
schnatternd, und warten im Dunkel,
den Säugling an die Rippen gepreßt,
in der Hand den Kanarienvogel,
auf die Sirenen, das Schlauchboot,
das ferne Schwirren des Hubschraubers.

4

What silken train, this population
of shiny ribs, flakes and veils,
how hurriedly they billow up, those banks,
bales, drums, domes and turrets, and then again
they stall, hang heavy for weeks,
grey and morose – progress
does not occur in the evolution
of clouds. Not a trace
of the fight for survival!
A pinch of dust is enough,
some salt or smoke.
Then they steam,
discharge, pour, flash, hail and snow.
Indeed, they mutate incessantly, over night,
resourceful creatures, non-violent.
No end to their variations, and yet
everything remains as it was.

5

But they have another face too.
Out of anger or exuberance
they bunch together, fist-clenching clusters,
threatening. Exploding in gall-like blackness
the old force erupts from them.
Suddenly everything cracks: sound,
tension, water and ice.

We're caught unawares in our beds
as usual, flee onto the roofs,
teeth chattering, and wait in the dark
with the infant pressed to our chest,
with cage and budge in our hands,
for the sirens, the rubber dinghy,
the helicopter's distant whirr.

6

Leider, mit ihrem Leumund
steht es nicht zum besten.
Es sei kein Verlaß auf sie, heißt es.
Wo sie endeten, wo sie anfingen,
nicht einmal das wisse man genau.
Dieses ewige Schwimmen, Verschwimmen
Thermik, Taupunkt und Turbulenz –,
grenzenlos leicht fertig sei das
und leicht verderblich.
Was wiegen sie überhaupt?
Das sei die Frage.
Auch daß sie ohne uns auskommen,
die Wolken, aber nicht umgekehrt,
mißfällt. Schwere Vorwürfe,
zu schwer vielleicht,
für das was so schwebend lebt.

7

Wehe uns, wenn sie frösteln!
In ihrem undurchsichtigen Innern
erzeugen sie dieses weiße Zeug,
Myriaden von zart verzweigten Dendriten,
eisig, ein jeder von jedem verschieden,
wie wir, doch vollkommen regelmäßig.

Kepler hatte kein Mikroskop,
doch er wußte Bescheid,
sah das Atomgitter, erriet
seine Rotationssymmetrie,
sechzig Grad, berechnete
seine Packungsdichte: $\pi / 2\sqrt{3}$.

Sublime Kristalle. Das Hinfällige
ist es, was winzig, unmerklich leicht,
auf unsere Häupter fällt
und, während wir schlafen,
tonnenschwer unter sich
manches, was atmet, begräbt.

6

Sadly, they don't have
the best reputation.
They're unreliable, it is said.
That there's no knowing even
where they end and where they begin.
Forever this floating and blurring –
thermal, dew point, turbulence –
how infinitely thoughtless, it is said,
and quick to corrupt.
What do they weigh at all?
That is the question.
Moreover, the clouds can
do without us, but not vice versa,
so there's disapproval. Grave accusations,
too grave, perhaps,
for that which lives without gravity.

7

Woe betide us, when they shiver!
In their opaque innards
they produce this white stuff,
myriads of filigree dendrites,
icy, each one different from each other,
as we are, but perfectly regular.

Kepler had no microscope,
but he knew his way,
saw the atomic grid, guessed
its rotational symmetry,
sixty degrees, calculated
its packing density: $\pi / 2\sqrt{3}$.

Sublime crystals. Frailty itself,
tiny, imperceptibly light,
falls on our heads
and, as we sleep, it will
bury many a thing that breathes
under its tons of weight.

8

»Nie kann das Meer der Lüfte
den echten Naturforscher kalt lassen«,
sagte sich einst Mr Howard,
der am Tottenham Green
seine Pillen drehte,
milden Anstalten zugeneigt.
Zum Aufklärer gereift
und zum Wolkenjäger,
brachte er, was am Himmel wehte,
entschieden in Ordnung:
Haarlocken, Schichten und Haufen,
bestimmte das Unbestimmte,
und schränkte es ein, »wodurch
die Gegenstände gestempelt werden«.
Doch auch lateinisch getauft
fahren sie fort, zu tun,
was sie wollen, die Wolken,
keine der andern gleich,
niemandes Mündel. Schwierig,
den Himmel zu stempeln. Ach,
nicht unbedingt, braver Howard,
ist es dir zu verdanken,
daß es aufklart, zuweilen.

9

Dann wieder hangen sie
über uns, zäh, wochenlang,
und wir brüten in ihrem Schatten,
der, graumeliert, keinen Schatten wirft,
unzufrieden, bis endlich
die schläfrige Decke aufreißt,
föhnig, die Luft auf einmal
elektrisch geistert, so,
daß wir aus dem Haus stürzen,
tänzelnd im hellen Taumel
unsrer Geschäfte, während dort oben
die Himmelskünstler, endlich,
wie wir, aus der Apathie erwacht,
ihre selbstlose Vorstellung geben.

8

'The ocean of air can never be to the Naturalist
a subject of unfeeling contemplation,'
said Mr Howard long ago,
while he was weighing pills and powders
on Tottenham Green,
a man inclined to mildness.
Mature, a man of the Enlightenment
and a hunter of clouds, he determinedly
put whatever swept across the sky
in order:
curls, layers and heaps;
he defined the undefined
and limited it, thereby
'putting a stamp on the objects'.
But even christened in Latin,
they continue to do
as they please, the clouds,
not one like the other,
subject to no one. It is difficult
to put a stamp on the sky. Oh,
it is not necessarily
thanks to you, good Howard,
that it clears up, occasionally.

9

Then again they hang low
above us, heavy, for weeks,
and we sit and ponder in their shadow,
that, shot with grey, casts no shadow,
unhappy, until at last
the sleepy blanket parts,
a warm wind blows, all of a sudden
the air is full of electric spirits, and we
rush out of our houses,
prancing in the reeling brightness
of our dealings, while up there
the artists of the sky, at last
awake after long apathy,
deliver their selfless performance.

10

Wir, die wir uns ängstlich fragen,
wie wir wieder runterkommen
mit unsern lachhaften Luftschiffen,
schwerfälligen Blechschachteln,
dröhnend vor Nervosität –
dagegen diese riesenhaften Nomaden!
Wüstenscheu wandern sie, leicht,
lentissimo maestoso,
über den Erdboden hin,
lassen sich treiben, gelassen,

und manchmal versammeln sie sich
zu Palavern, die schweigsam verlaufen.
Dann wieder wehen sie auseinander,
und langsam verdunsten sie in der Höhe,
bis nur noch eine einzige, klein

wie eine sehnsüchtige Erinnerung,
weiß am Himmel verweilt.

11

Über Fehler sind sie erhaben.
Daß eine von ihnen mißraten wäre,
wird so leicht niemand behaupten.
Was da in einer Minute niederprasselt,
sind Millionen von Graupeln.
Jede einzelne ist perfekt.
Kein Blitz, der dem andern gliche.
Und das alles ohne Gehirn!

Herzlos/herzig, arm/reich, gut/böse:
Probleme, die ihnen fernliegen.
Taifune, Sintfluten, Hagelschlag,
ihr sprachloses Schauspiel,
ein Jammer für manchen Mann,
sieht anders, ganz anders aus,
vor Bewunderung sprachlos vom
Ararat aus betrachtet.

10

We wonder anxiously
how we'll get down again
with our ludicrous air ships,
clumsy tin cans,
booming with nervousness—
unlike those gigantic nomads!
Desert shy they wander, lightly,
lentissimo maestoso,
above the ground,
drift along, unflustered,

and sometimes they gather
for palavers of great silence.
Then again they blow apart,
evaporate slowly high above,
and only a single cloud, small

as a yearning memory,
holds out, white, in the sky.

11

They are above mistakes.
No one will be quick to claim
that one of them is misshapen.
A minute-long shower
sends down millions of sleet flakes.
Every one is perfect.
No two flashes of lightning alike.
And all this without a brain!

Heartless/heartfelt, poor/rich, good/bad:
Those problems are alien to them.
Typhoons, deluges, hailstorms,
their wordless drama
means heartbreak for some,
but looks different, very different,
to the speechless admirer
watching from Ararat.

12

Eine Minute lang nicht hingeschaut,
schon sind sie da, plötzlich, weiß,
blühend ja, aber wenig handfest –
ein wenig Feuchtigkeit, hoch oben,
etwas Unmerkliches, das auf der Haut
hinschmilzt: rasanter Übergang
von Phase zu Phase – schön und gut.
Doch auch die Physik der Wolken
hat nicht alles im Griff.
Im Zweifelsfall »nimmt man an«,
»ist der Auffassung«. Schleierhaft,
diese Regengallen, Fallstreifen,
Lichtsäulen, Halos. Weiß der Himmel,
wie sie es machen. Eine Spezies,
vergänglich, doch älter als unsereiner.

Nur daß sie uns überleben wird
um ein paar Millionen Jahre
hin oder her, steht fest.

12

One moment of inattention,
and there they are, suddenly, white,
blossoming, indeed, but not very solid,
a bit of moisture, high above,
something imperceptible, melting
on the skin: rapid transition
from one phase to the next – all good and well.
But even the physics of clouds
is not entirely in control.
In case of doubt 'it is assumed',
'one is of the opinion'. They are opaque,
those broken rainbows, virga,
columns of light, halos. Heaven knows
how they do it. A separate species,
transient, but older than our kind.

And it will survive us by
plus minus a few million
years, that much is certain.

Hans Magnus Enzensberger was born in 1929 in the Bavarian town of Kaufbeuren, and grew up in Nazi Nuremberg. He studied German literature, philosophy and languages at the Universities of Elangen, Freiburg im Breisgau and Hamburg, and in Paris at the Sorbonne, completing his doctorate in 1955 with a thesis on the poetics of Clemens Brentano. At Freiburg the philosopher Martin Heidegger was an influential figure, but Enzensberger found him 'disagreeably authoritarian'. He then worked as a radio editor in Stuttgart until 1957.

Like all his books, his first collection, *defence of the wolves* (1957), provoked wildly differing reactions, with one reviewer calling his poetic critique of postwar Germany an 'unintentional parody of poetry', while another saw it as 'the first great political poetry since Brecht' from Germany's first 'angry young man'. He has always been a controversial figure in Germany, managing to upset even his admirers, but 'that's how it should be. It's a sign of vitality. I would be disappointed if there were a lukewarm, benevolent indifference.'

He was a founder member of Group 47, a loose grouping of disaffected German intellectuals including Heinrich Böll and Günter Grass, generally viewed as the most influential movement after the war, although Enzensberger now talks of the group as 'a historical myth': 'It just so happened that after the war there were a few guys who felt uneasy about the country, to put it mildly. It was like living with an enormous corpse in the cupboard.' Franz-Josef Strauss famously called them *Schmeissfliegen* (blowflies): writers whose attacks on its political institutions seemed to risk damaging Germany's clean postwar image.

In 1960 he published his pioneering anthology, *Museum der modernen Poesie* (Museum of modern poetry), introducing German readers to writers such as William Carlos Williams, Fernando Pessoa and Lars Gustafsson, but also expressing in his title his view that Modernism was defunct. In 1965 he founded the radical periodical *Kursbuch* (Railway Timetable), which published critical texts on the media and language and became a legendary forum for the student movement. In 1980 he founded the journal *Transatlantic*, and in 1985 began editing the prestigious book series *Die andere Bibliothek*, now featuring over 250 titles, among them *The watermark of poetry, or The art and enjoyment of reading poems* (1985) by one Andreas Thalmayr. He used the same pseudonym for *Poetry gets on my nerves! First aid for stressed readers* (2004), a playfully ironic guide to the subject for younger readers in the spirit of his *Poetry Machine* installation (2000) – which caused something of a stir in Germany when he demonstrated how it could churn out lines of 'poetry' at the touch of a button. 'Some of the poems are quite enjoyable,' he told a journalist. 'So I made a remark that was not well taken by some poets. I said anybody who can't do better than the machine should put away their pen.'

From 1961 he spent long periods abroad, living in Norway, Italy and the USA as well as West Berlin, before settling in Munich in 1979, where he still lives. He has also travelled to Mexico, South America, the Soviet Union, China and the Near East. A year in Cuba, in 1969 – where Castro denounced him as a CIA agent – inspired his master work, *The Sinking of the Titanic* (1978). He has translated poetry from English, French, Spanish, Italian, Swedish and Norwegian, and his own work has been translated into many languages. He has received numerous prizes and honours, including the Georg Büchner Prize (1963), Ernst Robert Curtius Prize (1997) and Heinrich Heine Prize (1998) in Germany, as well as Italy's Premio Bollati and the Spanish Premio Príncipe de Asturias.

His poetry's social and moral criticism of the post-war world owes much to Marxism, yet insists on the freedoms which have often been denied by Communist governments; like Orwell he maintains that satire and criticism should not be party-political. His introduction to English readers came with a Penguin *Selected Poems* in 1968. His *New Selected Poems* (2015) was expanded from his 1994 Bloodaxe *Selected Poems* to include poems from three later collections.

Enzensberger's books include several on culture and politics which have been translated into English, among these *Europe, Europe* (1989), *Mediocrity and Delusion* (1992) and *Civil War* (1994), as well as two bestselling works for young people, *The Number Devil* (1998), an entertaining look at maths, and *Where Were You, Robert?* (2000), about history. His most recent titles include *Hammerstein oder Der Eigensinn* (2008; *The Silences of Hammerstein*, University of Chicago Press, 2009), *Enzensbergers Panoptikum: Zwanzig Zehn-Minuten-Essays* (2012), *Herrn Zetts Betrachtungen* (2013; *Mr Zed's Reflections*, Seagull Books, 2015), and *Tumult* (2014).